Nick L

Billy Wonderful

Methuen Drama

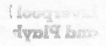

Published by Methuen Drama 2009

1 3 5 7 9 10 8 6 4 2

Methuen Drama
A & C Black Publishers Limited
36 Soho Square
London W1D 3QY
www.methuendrama.com

ISBN 978 1 408 11561 9

A CIP catalogue record for this book is available from
the British Library

Typeset by Country Setting, Kingsdown, Kent CT14 8ES
Printed and bound in Great Britain by
CPI Cox and Wyman Ltd, Reading RG1 8EX

**Liverpool Everyman
and Playhouse present
the world première of**

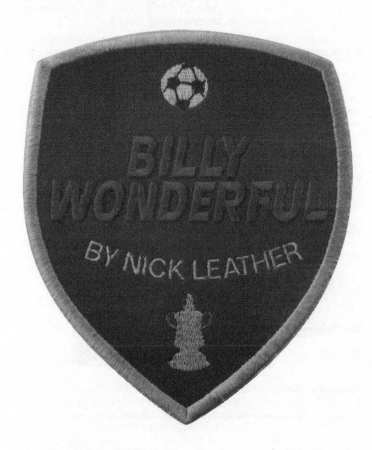

**First performed at the
Everyman Theatre, Liverpool
on 12 March 2009**

Sponsored by

**0151 709 4776
WWW.EVERYMANPLAYHOUSE.COM**

About the Theatres

Two Great Theatres. One Creative Heart.

Liverpool Everyman and Playhouse together make up a single engine for creative excellence, artistic adventure and audience involvement. Since 1999 the theatres have been on a remarkable journey, described as *"a theatrical renaissance on Merseyside"* Observer.

An integrated programme across the two buildings has generated critical acclaim and audience growth, and has been the springboard for forward-looking programmes of artist development and youth and community engagement. In less than five years the theatres have produced 20 world premières; audiences have grown by 47%; over 90,000 school and college students have participated in our work, and each year we have worked closely with over 10,000 people who had never been involved with theatre before.

Capital of Culture 2008 was a vitally important stage on the theatres' journey. It marked the end of the first cycle of development since the Everyman and Playhouse came together; but most importantly it now marks the beginning of a new cycle for the theatres and for the city. To find out more about our work, both on and off stage, call 0151 709 4776 or visit www.everymanplayhouse.com.

We Would Like to Thank

Our Funders

Our Sponsors

Corporate Members The Mersey Partnership, Uniform, EEF North West, DWF, Brabners Chaffe Street, Duncan Sheard Glass, 7 Harrington Chambers, Barbara McVey, Benson Signs, Grant Thornton, Downtown Liverpool in Business, Hope Street Hotel, Mando Group, Morgenrot Chevaliers plc, Synergy, Victor Huglin Carpets, Beetham, Chadwick LLP, Morecroft Solicitors, A C Robinson and Associates Ltd, Concept Communications, Kirwans Solicitors.

Trusts and Foundations The PH Holt Charitable Trust, The Liverpool Culture Company, The Rex Makin Charitable Trust, Malcolm and Roger Frood in memory of Graham and Joan Frood, Riverside Charitable Trust, Liverpool Housing Trust, Liverpool East Neighbourhood Management Services, CDS / Plus One, South Central Neighbourhood Management Services, Arena Housing, Isle of Man Arts Council, Unity Trust, Mary Webb Trust, Robert Kiln Trust, Margaret Guido Trust, N. Smith Charitable Trust, Elizabeth Jolly Charitable Trust, Rhododendron Trust, Wethered Bequest, J K Foundation, E Alec Colman Charitable Fund Ltd, Duchy of Lancaster Benevolent Fund, Constance Green Foundation, Elizabeth Margaret Susan Cotton Charitable Trust, Gilchrist Educational Trust, Eleanor Rathbone Charitable Trust, Helen Hamlyn Charitable Trust, Hemby Trust, Fenton Arts Trust, John Lewis Liverpool, donation in memory of Adrian Pagan.

This theatre has the support of the Pearson Playwrights' Scheme sponsored by Pearson plc.

And our growing number of individual supporters

Credits

Cast (in alphabetical order)

Bill Senior and ensemble	**Neil Caple**
Moz and ensemble	**Rob Law**
Shiner and ensemble	**Michael Ledwich**
Billy	**David Lyons**
MC and ensemble	**Shaun Mason**

Company

Writer	Nick Leather
Director	Serdar Bilis
Designer	Hannah Clark
Movement Director	Dan O'Neill
Lighting Designer	Ian Scott
Sound Designer	Kal Ross
Costume Supervisor	Jacquie Davis
Dramaturg	Suzanne Bell
Assistant Director	Rachel Littlewood
Production Manager	Kal Ross
Company Stage Manager	Paul Sawtell
Stage Manager	Natalia Cortes
Assistant Stage Manager on the Book	Helen Wilson
Stage Crew	Ian Davies

Cast

Neil Caple
Bill Senior and ensemble

Neil's theatre credits include:
Unprotected (Liverpool Everyman
and *Traverse*, Edinburgh); *The
Flint Street Nativity, Breezeblock
Park* and *The Odd Couple* (Liverpool
Playhouse); *Lost Soul* and *Two*
(Royal Court, Liverpool); *Othello*
(Watermill Theatre Company
& Tokyo); *The Merry Wives Of
Windsor, The Wind In The Willows,
The Trackers Of Oxyrynchus*
and *Strangeways* (Royal National
Theatre); *A Comedy Of Errors*
and *Macbeth* (Royal Shakespeare
Company).

Television credits include:
*Far From The Madding Crowd,
Cadfael* and *The Bullion Boys*.

Rob Law
Moz and ensemble

**Rob recently graduated from
Italia Conti and his credits include:**
*Bleak House, A Doll's House,
The Mysteries* and *Happy End.*

Theatre credits include: *Happy
End* (Chelsea Theatre), and
Scrooge (Bath Egg Theatre).

Michael Ledwich
Shiner and ensemble

Michael's theatre credits include:
Soul In The City (Neptune Theatre);
Somewhere, Lunch Hour and
If Trees Could Talk (Arts Centre);
Lord of the Flies (Tour); *Three
Sisters, My Favourite Year* and
Lear (Lipa); *On The Shore of the
Wide World* (Black Room); *The
Permanent Way* (Unity Theatre)
and *Once Upon A Time At The
Adelphi* (Liverpool Playhouse /
Trafalgar Studios)

Television credits include:
BBC'S *Liverpool Nativity,
Hearts and Minds, Chasing Amy*
and *Hollyoaks.*

Film Credits include: *Under
the Mud, Everywhere Doors*
and *After Morning After.*

David Lyons
Billy

David's theatre credits include:
Cherry Docs (King's Head Theatre),
Ten Tiny Toes (Liverpool
Everyman), *The Good Hope,
Robin Hood, Cymbeline, The
Relapse, Old Time Music Hall,
The Cherry Orchard* and *Plasticine*
(East 15 Acting School).

Television credits include: Stuart
Gordon in *Brookside.*

Short Film credits include: *Locket.*

Company

Shaun Mason
MC and ensemble

Shaun's theatre credits include:
Aladdin (St Helens Theatre Royal),
Council Depot Blues and *Stags
And Hens* (Royal Court, Liverpool),
*Ragged Trousered Philanthropist,
Noel Chavesse V.C M.C and Bar*
(Liverpool Anglican Cathederal),
Gods' Gift, King Of Edge Hill,
and *Your Breath In The Air* (Unity,
Liverpool), *Of Mice And Men,
Pals* (Dingle Theatre) and Road
Safety T.I.E plays.

In previous years Shaun has been
a tour guide for the Shiverpool
ghost tours and has toured
the United Kingdom extensively
performing Education Theatre
with Tiny Giants productions.

Television Credits include:
Tommo in *Brookside.*

Film Credits include: *Outlaws,
Death Defying Acts, Revenger's
Tragedy, The Pool* and *Dead Drunk.*

Nick Leather
Writer

Nick Leather's debut play *All The
Ordinary Angels* won the Pearson
Award for Best New Play 2005 and
was produced on the main stage
of Manchester's Royal Exchange
Theatre in October and November
of that year. Since then his work
has included a screen adaptation
of Bernard Hare's memoir *Urban
Grimshaw And The Shed Crew* for
Passion Pictures, *The Domino Man
Of Lancashire* for BBC Radio 4,
A Northern Elegy for BBC Radio 3,
School Rules for Channel 4, and
an attachment at the Royal National
Theatre. Previously, he was
Playwright-in-Residence at the
Royal Exchange and is an Associate
Writer of the Liverpool Everyman.

He is currently writing a new play
for the Royal Exchange Theatre
and *Wednesdays With Strangers*
for BBC Radio 4, whilst developing
both a screen adaptation of Danny
Rhodes' novel *Asboville* for
BBC Television, and *Cottonopolis*,
a radio drama series for Red
Productions / BBC Radio Drama.

Serdar Bilis
Director

Serdar trained as an actor in
Istanbul before completing a
directing course at Middlesex
University and the Royal
National Theatre.

Serdar's directing credits include:
Proper Clever (Liverpool Playhouse),
The May Queen (Liverpool
Everyman) and *A Family Affair,
Tartuffe* and *Night Just Before
The Forests* (Arcola.)
Serdar was formerly Associate

Director at the Everyman and Playhouse and is now a part time Associate Director for the Arcola Theatre in London. He is also part of the British Council New Writing scheme in Istanbul.

Hannah Clark
Designer

Hannah trained in Theatre Design at Nottingham Trent University and in 2005, completed an MA in Scenography with distinction at Central School of Speech and Drama. She was a winner of the 2005 Linbury Biennial Prize for stage design.

Theatre designs include: *Hortensia and the Museum of Dreams* (Vanbrugh Theatre, RADA); *The Snow Queen* (West Yorkshire Playhouse); *Proper Clever* (Liverpool Playhouse); *Pequenasdelicias* (Requardt and Company, Greenwich Dance Agency); *Torn* (Arcola Theatre, London); *Roadkill Café Part Two* (Requardt and Company, Teatro Fondamenta Nuove, Venice / The Place, London); *House Of Agnes* (Paines Plough, Oval House Theatre, London); *Breakfast With Mugabe* (Theatre Royal Bath - Ustinov Studio); *The Cracks In My Skin* (Manchester Royal Exchange Studio); *Roadkill Café Part One* (Requardt and Company, Centro Coreográfico de Montemor-o-Novo, Portugal); *Othello* (Salisbury Playhouse); *As You Like It, We That Are Left* (Watford Palace Theatre); *Who's Afraid Of Virginia Wolf?* (Royal Exchange Theatre, Manchester); *Big Love* (Gate Theatre, Notting Hill); *Terre Haute* (Assembly Rooms, Edinburgh / Trafalgar Studio 2 / UK Tour /

59E59 Theatres, New York); *Jammy Dodgers* (Requardt and Company, The Place, London / Royal Opera House 2, Clore Studio / INT Tour); *The Taming Of The Shrew* (Bristol Old Vic); *Death Of A Salesman, What The Butler Saw, Blue / Orange, A View From The Bridge, I Just Stopped By To See the Man, Two and Frankie* and *Johnny In The Clair De Lune* (Octagon Bolton).

Future work includes: *Under Milk Wood* (Northampton Theatre Royal); *Thyestes* (Arcola Theatre, London).

Dan O'Neil
Movement Director

On completing his dance training in London and New York, Dan enjoyed an extensive and varied dance career, working in both the funded and commercial sectors.

He performed with Toronto Dance Theatre, Extemporary and DV8, before becoming a founding member of the award winning '*Featherstonehaughs*', as well as appearing in pop videos, operas and *West Side Story.*

Dan assisted on *Jesus Christ Superstar* and *Dr Doolittle* in the West End, before choreographing many opera and theatre productions including: *Monkey* (The Young Vic); *Red Red Shoes* (Unicorn Theatre); *Peepshow* (Frantic Assembly) and *Wolves In the Walls* (National Theatre of Scotland).

He has written and directed several short dance films including: *The Linesman* (BBC/NPS), *Lapse* (Arts Council) and *Showtime*

(South East Arts). Dan teaches at both RADA and Central School of Speech and Drama.

Ian Scott
Lighting Designer

Recent credits include: *The Snow Queen* (West Yorkshire Playhouse); *Hansel and Gretel* (Northern Stage); *Proper Clever* (Liverpool Playhouse); *They're Playing Our Song* (Menier Chocolate Factory); *If You Were Me* (Library Theatre); Static (Suspect Culture and Graeae); and *The 39 Steps* (Criterion Theatre).

Other theatre credits include: *Oh What A Lovely War* (National Theatre); *Sinner* (Stan Won't Dance); *Eight Miles High* and *On the Ledge* (Royal Court Liverpool); *Our Friends In The North* (Northern Stage); *Blasted* (Graeae); *People At Sea* (Salisbury Playhouse); *Duck!* (Unicorn Theatre); *Dancing At Lughnasa* (Lyric Belfast); *Knots* (CoisCeim Dance Theatre); *The May Queen* (Liverpool Everyman); *Observe The Sons Of Ulster Marching Towards The Somme* (Abbey Theatre); *Timeless* (Suspect Culture); *Child Of The Divide* (Tamasha); *Dysfunction* (Soho Theatre); *Unheimlich Spine* (David Glass Ensemble); *Frogs* (Nottingham Playhouse); *Caledonia Dreaming* (7:84); *Two Step* (Push@Almeida); *Henry IV Part One* (The Peacock Dublin); *Crazy Horse* (Paines Plough) and *Stalinland* (Citizens Theatre).

Kal Ross
Sound Designer

Kal began his career as a recording studio engineer for Willy Russell.

He then went on to study acoustics in Manchester.

Sound designs and installations include: *The Quiet Little Englishman* (Zho Visual Theatre); *The Market Of Optimism; Lullaby Of Shadows* (BBC Radio 3); *My Psychotic Heart* and *The Singing Playwrights* (Willy Russell and Tim Firth); *Love Me Tonight* (Hampstead Theatre); *Sergeant Pepper's Magical Mystery Trip, Thick As A Brick* and *Gold* (Hull Truck); *The Corrupted Angel* (Bass Chorus); *The Starving Brides* (HUB) and *Ballad Of The Sea* (Landing Stage).

Kal has designed sound for many Everyman and Playhouse productions including: *Educating Rita, Romeo And Juliet, Popcorn, The Play What I Wrote, Oliver Twist, Treasure Island, Les Liasons Dangereuses, Alice In Boogie Wonderland, A Christmas Carol, The Lonesome West, Puss In Blue Suede Boots, Brothers Of The Brush, The Knocky, Happy Valley* and *Scouse*.

Kal has also worked extensively in TV and was production sound engineer on *Chicago* (UK and International Tour) as well as working UK arena tours and internationally on many other theatre and rock'n'roll shows.

Jaquie Davis
Costume Supervisor

Jacquie's theatre credits include: *Mother Goose, Endgame, Eric's, Intemperance, The Way Home, The Morris* and *Port Authority* (Liverpool Everyman); *Our Country's Good, Tartuffe, Once*

Upon A Time At The Adelphi
(Liverpool Playhouse); *Vurt, Wise
Guys, Unsuitable Girls* and *Perfect*
(Contact Theatre, Manchester);
Oleanna and *Memory* (Clwyd Theatr
Cymru); *Love On The Dole* (Lowry);
Never The Sinner (Library Theatre)
and *Shockheaded Peter* (West End).

Opera includes work at: Scottish
Opera, Buxton Opera Festival,
Music Theatre Wales and Opera
Holland Park.

Television and film includes:
*Queer as Folk, The Parole Officer,
I Love The 1970's* and *1980's,
Brookside* and *Hollyoaks*.

....

Rachel Littlewood
Assistant Director

Rachel trained at University of
Manchester gaining a first class
degree in 2004. Since then Rachel
has worked in theatres across
the North West including Contact
Theatre and the Liverpool Everyman
and Playhouse Theatres. Her
work spans from working with
very diverse communities to
professional actors.

Film Directing credits include:
Memory, Movement Message,
and *Communities On The Edge*
(River Media).

Theatre Credits include: *By the
Rivers,* (Liverpool Playhouse) and
Cruel Sea (Liverpool Everyman) -
both as assistant director.
In 2008, Rachel directed her first
professional theatre production
The Long And Winding Road
at the Liverpool Arts Centre.

....

The Company wishes to thank

TARGETSPORTS, British Military
Fitness, Mike McCann, Dolphin
Dance Studios, Stephen Done
and Debbie Bristow at Liverpool
Football Club and Marie Martin
and Dave Berry at Everton Football
Club for their help, patience and
co-operation.

Staff

Leah Abbott Box Office Assistant, **Vicky Adlard** Administrator, **Deborah Aydon** Executive Director, **Xenia Bayer** Technician, **Lindsey Bell** Technician, **Suzanne Bell** Literary Manager, **John Biddle** Admin Assistant, **Gemma Bodinetz** Artistic Director, **Pauline Bradshaw** Cleaning Staff, **Alec Burgess** Foyer Attendant, **Moira Callaghan** Theatre and Community Administrator, **Rebbecca Conneely** Box Office Manager, **Emily Crawford** Communications Assistant, **Jacquie Davies** Costume Supervisor, **Stephen Dickson** Finance Assistant, **Angela Dooley** Cleaning Staff, **Luke Dowdall** Box Office, **Sarah Ellis** Stage Door Receptionist, **Roy Francis** Maintenance Technician, Rosalind Gordon Deputy Box Office Manager, **Mike Gray** Deputy Technical Stage Manager, **Helen Grey** Assistant House Manager, **Helen Griffiths** House Manager, **Poppy Harrison** Box Office Assistant, **Stuart Holden** IT and Communications Manager, **Andy Irvine** Admin Assistant / Duty Manager, **David Jordan** Fire Officer, **Sarah Kelly** Assistant House Manager, **Sue Kelly** Cleaning Staff, **Steven Kennett** Assistant Maintenance Technician (Performance), **Sven Key** Fire Officer, **Andrew King** Box Office Assistant, **Rachel Littlewood** Community Outreach Co-ordinator, **Robert Longthorne** Building Development Director, **Esme Lowe** Creative Apprentice, **Howard Macaulay** Deputy Chief Technician (Stage), **Ged Manson** Cleaning Staff, **Christine Mathews-Sheen** Director of Finance and Administration, **Jason McQuaide** Technical Stage Manager (Playhouse), **Dan Meigh** Youth Theatre Director, **Gordon Millar** Producer, **Elizabeth Moran** Deputy Chief Electrician, **Gemma Murrell** Communications Officer – Services, **Liz Nolan** Assistant to the Directors, **Kim Norman** Finance Assistant, **Patricia O'Brien** Cleaning Staff, **Sarah Ogle** Communication and Sales Director, **Viv O'Callaghan** Youth Theatre Administrator, **Rowena Peers** Development Manager, **Katie Phipps** Stage Door Receptionist, **Danielle Piercy** Community Production Practitioner, **Sean Pritchard** Senior Production Manager, **Collette Rawlinson** Stage Door Receptionist, **Gary Rice** Bar Supervisor, **Lindsay Rodden** Literary Assistant, **Victoria Rope** Programme Manager, **Rebecca Ross-Williams** Theatre and Community Director, **Peter Ruddick** Communications Officer – Media, **Jeff Salmon** Technical Director, **Paul Sawtell** Company Manager, **Hayley Sephton** House Manager, **Steve Sheridan** Assistant Maintenance Technician, **Louise Sutton** Box Office Supervisor, **Jennifer Tallon-Cahill** Chief Electrician, **Pippa Taylor** Communications and PR Manager, **Marie Thompson** Housekeeper, **Amy Trego** Development Officer, **Scott Turner** Audience Insight Manager, **Paul Turton** Finance Manager, **Andrew Webster** Acting Chief Technician (Everyman), **Sarah Westhead** Foyer Attendant, **Emma Wright** Production Manager.

Thanks to all our Front of House team and casual Box Office staff.

Board Members

Cllr Warren Bradley, Professor Michael Brown (Chair), Mike Carran, Rod Holmes, Vince Killen, Professor E. Rex Makin, Andrew Moss, Paul Crewes, Jim Davies, Rosemary Hawley, Ivan Wadeson.

The regulations of Liverpool City Council provide that:

The public may leave at the end of the performance by all exit doors and all exit doors must at that time be open. Note: all Liverpool theatres can be emptied in three minutes or less if the audience leaves in an orderly manner.

All gangways, passages, staircases and exits must be kept entirely free from obstruction. Persons shall not be permitted to stand or sit in any of the intersecting gangways or stand in any unseated space in the auditorium unless standing in such space has been authorised by the City Council.

Smoking and drinking glasses are not allowed in the auditorium at any time.

We would like to remind you that the bleep of digital watches, pagers and mobile phones during the performance may distract the actors and your fellow audience members. Please ensure they are switched off for the duration of the performance. You are strongly advised not to leave bags and other personal belongings unattended anywhere in the theatre.

Billy Wonderful

With special thanks to all at
the Liverpool Everyman and Playhouse Theatres
for giving me the opportunity to write this play,
and supporting me throughout the process.

'Football is the opera of the people.'

Stafford Heginbotham, 1985

Bill Shankly once said that everything
he knew about life, he learnt from football.
Well, everything l know about football
I learnt from my Dad – so this is for him.

Notes on text and performance

An all-male cast is required.

The **Commentator** and **Summariser** can either be pre-recorded (preferably by voices that the audience is familiar with from television or radio), or created during the play by performers who are not playing primary characters during that particular scene.

Dialogue in *italics* is to be emphasised.

A dash (–) at the end of a speech indicates a point of interruption, and an ellipsis (. . .) indicates a trailing off.

A *pause* is longer than two *beats*.

The football strips worn by the cast should be from around the 1996/97 season.

The staging of the play should involve the creation of a football match before, during and after the performance – and turn the performance space, and the area around it, into a football stadium, and the area around that.

The audience should be divided into Liverpool and Everton fans – and given the option of purchasing tickets for either the Gladwys Street or Kop ends only. This is not a place for neutrals.

The audience should be encouraged to wear their colours.

The scenes do not interrupt the football match – rather they are part of it and the match is *always* in play. Consequently, **Crowd** noise and match atmosphere should play continually in the background and be brought to the fore when indicated in the text.

Songs, chants and shouts from the **Fans** should be performed by any, or all, of the actors not playing a primary character in the particular scene.

Queen Jean's voice should also be delivered by the chorus of performers not playing a primary character in the particular scene.

Characters and Creations
Five male, in order of appearance for each performer:

IN EVERTON SHIRT
Billy, *eight to thirty*

IN LIVERPOOL SHIRT UNTIL STATED OTHERWISE
Street Evangelist, *sixties*
Golden Goal Seller, *late thirties*
Player, *late twenties*
Bill Sr, *thirty to fifty-two*
Fan, *forties*
Liverpool Full Back, *late twenties*
Tree
Pro-Evo Footballer
Puncture

IN EVERTON SHIRT UNTIL STATED OTHERWISE
Bluenose, *mid-teens*
MC, *early forties*
Subbuteo Footballer
Everton Captain, *late twenties*
Fan, *thirties*
Queen Jean, *late twenties*
Clifford, *eight*
Everton Boss, *mid-forties to late forties*
Liverpool Midfielder, *early twenties*
Hardman Johnny Dexter
Claire, *thirteen to twenty-seven*
Sailor, *early twenties*
Agent, *late thirties to mid-forties*
Physio, *late thirties*
Player, *late teens*
Pro-Evo Footballer
Everton Substitute, *early twenties*
Puncture

IN LIVERPOOL SHIRT UNTIL STATED OTHERWISE
Kopite, *mid-teens*
Bizzie, *mid-thirties*
Subbuteo Footballer

Liverpool Captain, *late twenties*
Fan, *twenties*
Queen Jean, *late twenties*
Shiner, *eight*
Everton Striker, *mid-twenties*
Blackie Gray
Line-Marker
Elaine, *thirteen to twenty-nine*
Tree
Sailor, *early twenties*
Youth Coach, *mid-fifties*
Fourth Official, *forties*
New Boss, *early forties*
Pro-Evo Footballer
Boy, *seven*
Liverpool Substitute, *early twenties*
Puncture

IN REFEREE'S SHIRT
Bookie, *mid-thirties*
Subbuteo Referee
Referee, *early forties*
Fan, *teens*
Queen Jean, *late twenties*
Moz, *eight to thirty*
Roy Race
Tree
Shantyman, *mid-thirties*
Player, *late teens*
Boy, *nine*

Additionally: **Match-day Stewards** and a **Toffee Girl**

Setting

Thirty-year-old Billy Walters relives a Merseyside 'derby match'
that took place when he was nineteen years of age – the first
half telling the story of the eleven years that led up to this
game, and the second half the eleven that followed.

Pre-Match

Outside the performance space, as the **Crowd** *arrives, a* **Street Evangelist** *walks up and down the pavement with a banner proclaiming 'Prepare To Meet Thy God', while a* **Kopite** *and a* **Bluenose** *also approach members of the* **Crowd** *directly – repeating certain lines like a mantra.*

Street Evangelist   Many are called, but few are chosen! Many are called, but few are chosen!

Kopite   Mind yer car, mate? Can I mind yer car?

Bluenose   Eh, lad, any spares? Got any spares? Have yer?

Street Evangelist   Support Jesus, not the Reds or the Blues! He'll never let yer down! He'll never let yer lose!

Kopite   Payment up front! Cash accepted! No change given!

Bluenose   Tickets! Anybody lookin' for tickets? Get your derby ticks here! Shhhh. Just between us. Cos of your smile – only twenty to you. Alright then, call it fifteen. Last chance – a tenner with a Bovril thrown in!

Around the performance space, scarves, woolly hats and memorabilia from both Everton and Liverpool football clubs are available – as well as traditional refreshments such as Bovril, pies and hot dogs. A **Bookie** *tries to draw people to a board featuring the latest odds.*

Bookie   Liverpool one up at half-time and Everton to win two–one – I'll give ya forties, on my life. I'm deadly, I am. I blag thee not. Billy Walters, young William Walters, Billy Bluenose, Billy the Kid, Billy Whizz – fifty to one first goalscorer! Thirty-threes the winner! Come on, Bob Geldof couldn't beat that! More generous than Live Aid 'ere! Quick, whilst yer can, don't miss out – get your Bookie Aid 'ere! Receive generously! Free cash doled out by the handful at full-time!

As the **Crowd** *enter the performance space itself, a* **Golden Goal Seller** *and a* **Bizzie** *await them.*

Golden Goal Seller   Golden goal! Golden goal! Get your golden goals 'ere!

Bizzie   Any bottles? Cans? A flask? What's in your flask? Caf or decaf? Mind if I have a look in your bag? Only doin' me job. Crisps? What flavour?

Golden Goal Seller   Golden goal! Golden goal!

Bizzie   Tickets? Lemme see your tickets! Hold 'em in the air, come on. All juniors, cards at the ready. Need some ID. You're not under sixteen, lad, you're older than me!

Inside the performance space, all non-performers involved in the production are dressed as match-day **Stewards** *in luminous jackets, and the walls are draped with famous Everton and Liverpool banners of the past, along with the odd impostor: 'Beware the Dogs of War'; 'Kenny's from Heaven'; 'Billy Walters Walks on Water'; 'Shankly Lives Forever'; 'Sorry Elton – But I Guess That's Why They Call Us the Blues'; 'Joey Ate the Frogs' Legs, Made the Swiss Roll, and Now He's Munching Gladbach'; 'The Boys from the Blue Stuff'; and, biggest of all, 'We Are Not English, We Are Scouse'. Music is interrupted periodically as an* **MC** *strides onto the pitch with a microphone.*

MC   I've got a quick happy birthday 'ere for a Harrison Roberts. Harrison's two and today's his first derby match. (*Beat.*) What took yer, Harrison lad?

The **Players** *start to warm up on the pitch.*

MC   I've got a message 'ere from a Julie from Bootle. No surname. She's a Bluenose and she's here today with her boyfriend Gary, who's a Red. Julie'd like to say, 'Gary, I love you very much. You mean the world to me. Will you marry me?' (*Beat.*) I'll give that one ninety minutes max. Quickest divorce in history . . .

A **Toffee Girl** *throws sweets into the crowd.*

MC   I've just been handed today's team sheets and the big news is that on the bench for Everton for the first time is Billy Walters. Billy's only nineteen and he's a local lad, so all the best, Billy boy, all the best. Break a leg, or even better – break one o' theirs. Just a joke, folks, just a joke.

When the stands are full, 'Johnny Todd' – the theme tune from Z-Cars – *should start to play.*

And the players are in the tunnel, ladies and gentlemen. Bragging rights in the city are about to be decided for the next few months, so make some noise and please show your appreciation for . . . Everton . . . and . . . Liverpool!

First Half

One   EVERTON 0 – LIVERPOOL 0

Billy Walters, *aged thirty, crouches opposite an older man,* **Bill Sr**, *in the living room of a high-rise flat.* **Subbuteo Footballers** *are in between them. As the* **Subbuteo Referee** *blows his whistle, a* **Crowd** *roars and* **Billy** *and* **Bill Sr** *look at each other.*

Bill Sr   Right?

Billy   Right!

They flick their **Subbuteo Footballers**, *who – along with the* **Subbuteo Referee** *– immediately leap from their bases and charge after the ball.*

Commentator   The one hundred and eighty-sixth Merseyside derby is under way! This is not a place for neutrals. For the next ninety minutes this city will be split into two – families torn apart and friends turned into enemies. From here on in, you're either a Red or a Blue. Which are you?

The **Liverpool Captain** *and the* **Everton Captain** *clatter into each other.*

Commentator   Ouch! What a start!

The **Crowd** *erupts and the* **Referee** *blows his whistle over and over again.*

Everton Captain   Referee!

Liverpool Captain   Referee!

Billy *looks at the* **Referee**, *then the* **Everton Captain**, *the* **Liverpool Captain**, *and finally the* **Crowd**.

Everton Captain   Get him in the book!

Liverpool Captain   Never touched him!

Commentator   Both teams came into the game suffering from injuries and suspensions – will anyone be left standing come the final whistle? It won't be a game for the faint-hearted, that's for sure . . .

As **Bill Sr** *continues to flick his* **Subbuteo Footballers**, **Billy** *watches the action and starts to breathe heavily.*

Bill Sr   I'm hammerin' you 'ere, Billy lad!

Referee   Calm down, boys. I'm runnin' the show.

Commentator   Any predictions?

Summariser   Well, the form book really goes out of the window in a derby match. Too . . . close . . . to . . . call.

Commentator   One thing's for sure, folks – if your phone rings, don't answer it. If there's a knock on the door, ignore it. You won't want to miss a kick of this one. This could be the game –

Summariser   This could be the game –

Commentator   The game –

Summariser   The game –

Billy   The game . . . of a lifetime.

The **Fans** *in the stand inhale collectively and suddenly* **Billy** *leaps up and faces the crowd.*

Billy   I don't believe in God. Not really. Mean I'd like to, I would, but bad things happen to good people, don't they, so the jury has to be out for me. Don't believe in Religion at all TBH cos things get twisted and wrong can look right. And I don't believe in Everlastin' Life cos I'm gettin' older, aren't I, and the gettin' older's gettin' quicker, and vrrroooom – reckon in the blink of an eye I'll be a goner prob'ly so there ya go. I don't believe in that Atheism either though cos it takes too much faith. Mean it's a nice story, ain't it, but a bit far-fetched like, eh? And Reincarnation? Have I got a problem with that. What if I came back as a Kopite? Not havin' that. No way. Uh-uh. And I don't believe in your Freedom and Equality and shite like that cos some people are scummy let's be honest. Some people are really 'orrible and they just oughta be locked up and the key thrown away whether they've done anythin' or not. And I tell ya what, I don't believe in Politics or Politicians, cos they're all the same to me – and the only thing they believe in . . . is themselves. And Global Warmin'? I don't believe in that. I mean, why all the palaver? Just send the polar bears over some armbands and Triple-X Speedos. Nah, I leave my telly on standby out o' principal. I'd bash up a fridge for kicks. They reckon things are so bad that now even the sunshine's turned against us. Well, if it drops out o' the sky, no panic here – I'll just take it down on my chest and volley it right back through that big hole in the ozone. Bang! Get in! (*Beat.*) I don't believe in Conspiracy Theories at all. I think things are as they seem, don't you? I think your man Oswald shot JFK. On his own. End o' story. Grassy knoll? My fat arse! I think Elvis *is* dead. I think Elvis *was* shite. And I think he *is* dead, right? I think the Scottish Tourist Board invented the Loch Ness Monster just like Coca-Cola cooked up Santa. All my prezzies came from a bloke in red and white alright, but it was me al' fellah not St Nick. Nah. Don't believe in any of 'em. And I deffo don't believe in me, cos I'm a proper knobhead, aren't I, and always have been. I mean, it's an awful big world, proper ginormous, and I'm only a little fellah. Is it any wonder I'm always losin' myself and tryna work out where I was when I last had me? No. Nah. No ways. Don't believe in any of it. But . . . there *is* one thing. One thing I believe in. One thing you can. I think . . . I really think . . . there *is* a thing. I believe . . . are yer listenin'? I do believe. I believe. In *football*.

The **Fans** *breathe out and the* **Crowd** *roars. His eyes returning to the action,* **Billy** *sits down. The* **Everton Captain** *and the* **Liverpool Captain** *battle for the ball once more, watched by the* **Referee**.

Commentator   And there on the Everton bench for the very first time is young Billy Walters. Only nineteen years of age. What a debut this would be! How d'you think he's feeling now?

Summariser   Terrified!

As **Billy** *continues to stare, he becomes:*

Two   EVERTON 0 – LIVERPOOL 0

Billy, *aged eight, staring out of the window of the Walters' new flat. On one side of him is a large box with 'Jean's stuff' written on it. On the other side of him,* **Bill Sr** *has a Subbuteo set out and is setting up the* **Subbuteo Footballers***, goal posts, stands, floodlights and more.*

Bill Sr   Come on, Billy lad, give us an 'and settin' up the Subbuteo.

Billy   No.

Bill Sr   Baggsies red, mate. I bagsies red, alright?

Billy   I-I wanna go home.

Bill Sr   This *is* home.

Billy   Isn't.

Bill Sr   Will be. Once we're settled in.

Billy *stares at the large box. Pause.*

Bill Sr   Let's just play, eh, Billy? Let's have a game. It's what we do, innit.

Billy   Too high up, this flat.

Bill Sr   Too high up? There's no such thing. Just imagine this block is the league table, mate. Our flat's headin' for the title!

Billy   I want a garden.

Bill Sr   You've got one. Down there. You can have that one. Look. That's not a park any more, that's yours. It's on me. All of it. The footie pitch, the trees, the lake, the –

Billy   There's more trolleys in there than Tesco's!

Fans (*chant*)
   What a load o' rubbish
   What a load o' rubbish!

Bill Sr   They aren't trolleys, they're . . . steppin' stones. Across the lake of . . . the magic lake. Yeah. And this is an enchanted castle and, um –

Billy   Dad.

Bill Sr   What?

Billy   You're not Mum.

Bill Sr (*beat*)   No. I know.

Billy   I can't remember what I had for t-tea the night before last.

Bill Sr   So?

Billy   Can you?

Bill Sr   Er . . . butties, I think, mate. Yeah. We had cheese butties.

Billy   What if we forget? What if we just forget her like I forgot the cheese butties?

Bill Sr   Billy, no way. No way. Trust me.

Billy   The cheese butties have just proper vanished out of my b-b-b-brain, honest.

Bill Sr   Billy, stop stutterin', will yer?! Just speak properly! It's easy enough. Why would yer wanna start doin' that?

Pause.

Sorry, mate. Look. Close your eyes.

Billy   No.

Bill Sr   Close 'em like she said.

Billy *closes his eyes. There is a pause, then:*

Queen Jean (*sings*)
   My friends say that we're heading for a grotty time
   It's just a load of slapstick in a pantomime
   We're heading for disaster, but I just don't care
   Shut your eyes and count to ten, you won't be there
   The whole thing's daft, I don't know why
   You have to laugh, or else you cry
   You have to live or else you die
   You have to laugh or else you cry.

Bill Sr   Can you hear her?

Billy *opens his eyes and nods.* **Bill Sr** *moves closer to him.*

Bill Sr   Billy, I . . . I can't just click my fingers and make everythin' better, y'know. I wish I could, but I can't. And I've got the knot in my stomach too. I've got that hum in my head. And when I think about what happens next, about . . . bein' thirty years old, about whether or not there is a life after footie, the knot gets knottier and the hum gets louder and louder – but this is still the place. This is where we have to be. Near your Auntie Mo and Uncle Terry and our Maurice. It's no good bein' on our own, is it? There will be no more away games, mate. That's it. That's . . . done. So let's not just sit 'ere rubbin' our bellies, eh, Billy? Let's not just sit 'ere stickin' our fingers in our ears. Let's play on, mate. Let's have a game.

Billy   I don't want to.

Bill Sr   Billy, please, mate. Please. Just have a game with me. Please.

Billy *doesn't move an inch away from the window.* **Bill Sr***'s head sinks. Pause.*

Billy   Dad?

Bill Sr   What?

Billy   D'yer think yer can see Heaven from here?

There is a pause, then **Bill Sr** *swipes his hands and scatters the* **Subbuteo Footballers***, then the* **Liverpool Full Back** *hoofs the ball up into the air.*

Commentator   Strong challenge! And it's up in the clouds that one!

The **Liverpool Captain** *jostles the* **Everton Captain** *as they position themselves for the aerial challenge, and* **Billy** *becomes:*

Three   EVERTON 0 − LIVERPOOL 0

Billy, *still aged eight, standing on the roof of the Walters' block of flats. Alongside him are* **Moz** *and two other boys,* **Shiner** *and* **Clifford**. *All are looking up at the sky.*

Billy   Moz! Yer said it'd make us sneeze!

Moz   It will, Billy, just wait!

Shiner   I had a sneeze yesterday. It was great.

Clifford   I think I've gone blind.

Billy   Liar.

Clifford   Who said that?

Moz   Are yis sure Uncle Bill won't get us done for bein' up 'ere on the roof, Billy?

Billy   He won't be home for ages, I told ya − he's got an interview.

Clifford   Is just colours. I can just see colours and shapes.

Moz   Shut up, Clifford!

Clifford   I'm gonna go there one day.

Shiner   Where?

Clifford   The sun.

Moz   No one can go the sun, divvy!

Clifford   Why not?

Moz   It's too hot, innit. It's like Alicante 'cept without the sea to cool ya down.

Clifford   The moon then.

Shiner   How yis gonna get to the moon, Clifford?

Clifford   Space rocket, innit. I am gonna be a spaceman.

Moz   I'm gonna be a footballer!

Billy Like me dad?

Shiner No, he's gonna be a good one!

Shiner and **Clifford** *kill themselves laughing.*

Billy Shut up, youse!

Moz You don't get paid for footie if you're rubbish, y'know!
My mam says me Uncle Bill was 'dependable'. That's what she
says. And 'versatile'. D'yer know what 'versatile' means?
Means even if he might not be very good, he can be not very
good in any position on the 'ole pitch.

Shiner Yeah, but you're trainin' with Liverpool and
Liverpool are better than Bournemouth, aren't they?

Clifford Is right.

Shiner And now he's goin' for an interview for a job, and
proper players don't go for interviews for jobs. I've been down
the doley with me dad and I ain't never seen John Barnes
there. Not once.

Billy Well . . . well . . . my mum was a star! She woulda
been. That's what everyone says. When she sung she made
people happy. They didn't call her Queen Jean for nothin'!

All the boys look uncomfortable at the mention of **Billy**'s *mum. There is
a pause, then* **Moz** *decides to fill the silence.*

Moz When I'm in the Liverpool first team me mam and dad
won't never argue. They won't never fall out. Not ever. I'll get
'em the best seats in the ground. And they'll be dead happy.
I'll get 'em seats for the dugout!

Clifford Ha! Mams and dads can't sit in the dugout, doofus!

Moz Mine'll be able to!

Shiner I'm gonna be an impressionist. Like . . . like, here's
my Prince Charles. 'Hello, Queen. Hello, Diana.'

Billy, **Moz** and **Clifford** *laugh raucously.*

Billy That's brilliant that, Shiner!

Moz   I'm gonna be sick! I'm gonna be sick!

Clifford   If you can't see it, it's like it's actually him.

Shiner   'Hello, Queen. Hello, Diana.'

Clifford (*bows*)   Your Majesty.

Billy   Ha!

Clifford   Do another one.

Shiner   Huh?

Clifford   Well, to be an impressionist you have to be able to do more than one impression.

Moz, **Billy** and **Clifford** *stare at* **Shiner**. *Pause.*

Shiner   Well, well, to be a spaceman you need to be dead good at maths!

Clifford   I am! I am! Ask me to add anythin'!

Shiner   You need to be able to divide.

Clifford   Oh.

Shiner   Not just anyone can drive a space rocket, y'know.

Clifford   I didn't wanna drive. I just wanted to look out the window.

Shiner   What d'you wanna be, Billy?

Clifford   Yeah, what d'you wanna be?

Billy *remains focused on the sun.*

Moz   Billy?

Bill Sr *bursts onto the roof.*

Bill Sr   What are you lot doin' up 'ere?! I've told yer!

Moz   Uncle Bill . . .

Bill Sr   Get off the roof! Now!

Shiner   Billy?

Billy   I wonder if . . .

Clifford   Billy?

Billy   I wonder if I'm a star . . .

Billy *sneezes.* **Shiner** *and* **Clifford** *cheer, the sun falls from the sky, and the* **Everton Captain** *and the* **Liverpool Captain** *leap the highest to challenge for the ball – accidentally clashing heads as they do so. They fall to the ground in agony.* **Billy** *watches.*

Referee   Physio! Physio!

Commentator   Oh! And a sickening clash of heads! There might have to be changes here. And with the Everton bench so threadbare, who will they bring on?

There is a pause, then **Billy** *starts to do stretches and becomes:*

Four   EVERTON O – LIVERPOOL O

Billy, *on his ninth birthday, fidgeting nervously in the living room of the Walters' flat.* **Bill Sr** *and* **Moz** *stare at him.* **Bill Sr** *is holding a wrapped present and a card.*

Bill Sr   Come on, Billy.

Moz   Open it, Billy.

Fan (*shouts*)   Get stuck in, Blues!

Bill Sr   Don't make a show of yourself, mate. Not on your birthday.

Billy   I'm not m-makin' a show of myself. Just don't want a birthday. Birthdays are rubbish.

Moz   Birthdays? Birthdays are brilliant! You're crackers you, Billy! There's no one else in the whole world who doesn't love birthdays! Birthdays are when everybody's happy and gets on and there's prezzies and cake and –

Billy   Where's my cake?

Bill Sr   Oh, right, yeah. Cake. Didn't think about cake.

Moz   You could make us a cake!

Bill Sr   Behave, Maurice lad.

Moz   I seen me mam do it, it's easy. Have yis got eggs in, Uncle Bill?

Bill Sr   Yeah.

Moz   Margarine?

Bill Sr   Yeah.

Moz   Flour?

Bill Sr   No.

Moz   We can't have cake, Billy, but we could have fried eggs.

Billy   I don't want fried eggs. You can't stick candles in fried eggs.

Bill Sr   Open your prezzie, mate, eh?

Billy   I don't want a prezzie off yer! Don't want anythin' off yer! You don't know what I want. You don't know what you should get. You don't even know to buy cake!

Fan (*shouts*)   And again, eh! And again!

Bill Sr   Billy, listen. I've got a bit o' good news. I've got a job. Liverpool have taken me on.

Moz   Wha'?!

Billy   You're gonna play for Liverpool?

Bill Sr   No, mate. No. As if. No. Groundsman.

Billy   Groundsman?

Bill Sr   Assistant actually. I'm gonna be workin' at Anfield. And I mean, that's great, innit. I mean, different – but good. Means I'll still be at home every night. Means I still get to run up and down the touchline. (*Beat.*) So open your card, eh, pal.

Billy   What's the point? I know what it says.

Bill Sr   What does it say?

Billy   Says, 'Happy Birthday, Billy. Dad.'

Pause.

Bill Sr   Doesn't say that.

Billy   What does it say then?

Bill Sr (*beat*)   The card and the prezzie . . . well . . . they're not from me. Not really. They're from . . . she got 'em, mate. I've had 'em months. They've been in the cupboard. y'know. Just waitin' for today.

Bill Sr *places the present in the middle of the room and backs away from it.* **Billy** *doesn't move.* **Moz** *feels awkward.*

Billy   Read it then.

Bill Sr   Eh?

Billy   Read it.

Billy *and* **Moz** *stare at* **Bill Sr**. **Bill Sr** *opens the envelope, takes the card out, looks at it for a moment, then clears his throat.*

Bill Sr   'Dear Billy.' (*Beat.*) 'It's difficult to know what to write. Hopefully the prezzie will say it all.'

Billy *looks at the present and starts to inch towards it. As he does so, the* **Fans** *start to hum the Piranhas' version of 'Tom Hark' – quietly at first, but increasing in volume.*

Bill Sr   'But listen, lad – if you work hard and always do your best then . . . then you can be a star, y'know. It'll be like it was with Latchford. It'll be painted on the walls of Walton. Billy Walters Walks on Water. Billy Walters Walks on Water. You can do it, Billy. You can. One day you'll score the winner in the derby. If you work hard and always do your best, then . . . then you *can* do it.'

Billy *grabs the present, and starts to rip the paper from it.* **Bill Sr** *breathes a sigh of relief.* **Moz** *starts to read the inside of the card, before* **Bill Sr** *hurriedly snatches it away from him and puts it back in the envelope.* **Moz** *and* **Bill Sr** *look at each other for a moment.*

Commentator   Is he bringing the young lad on?

Summariser   It'd be a risk, that's for sure.

Commentator   He is, y'know. Walters is getting stripped. He's getting ready.

Billy *pulls a football from the paper, clutches it to his chest and stares at it with determination. The humming stops as the* **Everton Boss** *puts a hand on his shoulder.*

Everton Boss   Walters, don't forget what I said yesterday, OK? You know what it's all about. Stay on that wing and get chalk on your boots. Run at 'em. Scare 'em. And don't let it pass you by . . .

Billy *nods, takes a deep breath, and holds the ball out.*

Commentator   Making his debut in this game of games is young Billy Walters – and what a gamble it is. This Everton manager's under real pressure at the moment. A last roll of the dice, perhaps?

Summariser   Three words. Baptism. Of. Fire.

The **Everton Boss** *takes the ball from him and* **Billy** *runs onto the pitch. The roar from the* **Crowd** *is deafening. As* **Billy** *starts to run, he becomes:*

Five   EVERTON 0 – LIVERPOOL 0

Billy, *aged ten, playing footie with* **Moz** *in the park.* **Billy** *is on the ball.*

Moz   Come on, Billy!

Commentator   And an early touch for Walters here.

Summariser   Bound to be a few butterflies . . .

Billy *looks up as a butterfly flutters by.*

Moz   Can't beat me! Can't beat me!

Billy I can! I can! Just watch!

Fan (*shouts*) That's it! Run at him! Run at him!

Billy *runs at* **Moz** *over and over again.*

Moz Never!

Billy I will!

Eventually, **Billy** *sells* **Moz** *the dummy and* **Moz** *goes sliding past him.* **Billy** *laughs.*

Billy Up yer get, Maurice!

Moz Was a fluke! Won't do it again!

And with that, **Billy** *and* **Moz** *resume their duel.* **Billy** *runs at the* **Liverpool Midfielder** *and beats him, but loses his balance as he closes in on the* **Liverpool Full Back***. As he stumbles to the turf, the* **Referee** *waves play on, and* **Billy** *becomes:*

Six EVERTON 0 − LIVERPOOL 0

Billy*, aged eleven, reading a copy of* Roy of the Rovers *in the living room of the Walters' flat.* **Bill Sr** *stands behind him.*

Bill Sr Billy? Are yer listenin' to me, lad?

Billy Dad, I'm readin' about Roy Race!

Bill Sr Yer bein' a lazy get, I know that.

Billy Roy Race is the greatest footballer what ever-ever lived.

Bill Sr He never lived, Billy. He's made up.

Billy *pulls the comic closer to him. There is a pause, then* **Hardman Johnny Dexter** *and* **Blackie Gray** *appear and move through the frames of a comic strip.*

Blackie Gray Billy?

Billy   Blackie Gray? And Hardman Johnny Dexter? You're Mellie Rovers legends! (*Thinks.*) Hmm, I wonder what they're doing here?

They move into the next frame.

Blackie Gray   We've been watching you, Billy.

Hardman Johnny Dexter   You've impressed the boss.

Billy   The boss? (*Thinks.*) Surely they don't mean . . .

As they move into the next frame, **Roy Race** *appears alongside them:*

Roy Race   Hello, Billy.

Billy   Roy Race!

They move into the next frame:

Roy Race   I've got something to ask you, Billy.

Billy (*thinks*)   I hope he wants me to play for Melchester!

Bill Sr   Billy!

They move into the next frame.

Roy Race   Billy . . .

Billy   Yes, Roy?

Bill Sr   Billy, I'm talking to you!

Roy Race, **Blackie Gray** *and* **Hardman Johnny Dexter** *start to disappear.*

Billy   I'm readin'!

Bill Sr   You're too old for comics! Isn't it time you grew up, eh?

There is a pause, then **Billy** *tries to regain his feet, but the* **Liverpool Full Back** *cleans out both ball and man, and emerges in possession.*

Commentator   That's knocked the wind out of his sails!

Summariser   He'll be OK. They're made of tough stuff up here, y'know!

Billy *gets up again, chases back after the* **Liverpool Full Back***, and becomes:*

Seven   EVERTON 0 − LIVERPOOL 0

Billy*, aged twelve, jogging across Anfield as* **Bill Sr** *marks the touchline with a* **Line-Marker***.*

Billy   Dad!

Bill Sr   Billy, what are yer doin'? I'm workin' . . .

Billy   I couldn't wait till you got home!

Bill Sr   I've still got half the pitch to get round.

Billy   The letter's come.

Bill Sr   I've not got time for −

Billy   About the trial.

Bill Sr   Oh . . . oh, right.

Billy *stops trailing after him, but* **Bill Sr** *continues to march along the touchline with the* **Line-Marker***.*

Bill Sr   Look, Billy − this is how it goes, mate. Look at me − markin' the lines rather than runnin' along 'em. This is just how it goes.

Billy   They're takin' me on.

Fans (*clap-clap-clap-clap-clap-clap*)   Ev-ton!

Bill Sr *turns slowly.*

Bill Sr   Everton are takin' you on?

Billy *nods.*

Commentator   The full back's in space . . .

Summariser   Needs to show a bit of composure . . .

Suddenly **Bill Sr** *starts to push the* **Line-Marker** *away from the touchline and onto the pitch.*

Billy   Dad! You'll ruin the grass!

Bill Sr   Bugger the grass!

Bill Sr *pushes the* **Line-Marker** *around in enormous squiggles and loops.*

Billy   What are yer doin'?

Bill Sr   I'm writin'!

Billy   Writin' what?

Bill Sr   'Wonderful', Billy! 'Wonderful'!

As **Bill Sr** *massacres the pitch,* **Billy** *harries player after player and slides in to win back possession . . .*

Fans (*sing*)
Can you hear the Kopites sing (no-oh, no-oh)
Can you hear the Kopites sing (no-oh, no-oh)
Can you hear the Kopites sing
I can't hear a bastard thing
Woh-oh, wo-oh-oh!

The ball runs loose to the **Everton Striker**. *As he clips it back to* **Billy**, **Billy** *becomes:*

Eight   EVERTON 0 − LIVERPOOL 0

Billy, *aged thirteen, training after school with* **Moz** *as two girls −* **Elaine** *and* **Claire** *− watch.* **Billy** *and* **Moz** *run from different directions, leaping at the same point and time to head an imaginary ball, before landing and continuing in different directions, until they touch the ground, swivel and do the same thing again in reverse: running, jumping, running, turning, running, jumping, running, turning. However, with each circuit,* **Moz** *becomes increasingly distracted by the girls.*

Elaine   Say hello to him then.

Claire   I'm not sayin' hello!

Elaine   Go on, Claire! Dares ya!

Claire   Shurrup, Elaine, he can hear!

Billy   Come on, Moz!

Elaine   Hey! Maurice Minor! Maurice Dancer!

Moz   Me name's not Maurice, it's Moz. And it's not Minor or Dancer, it's O'Connor. OK? Get it right.

Elaine   Why are youse two still 'ere? You're meant to go home after school, y'know.

Moz   Well, you're still here, aren't yer?

Elaine   Only cos Claire's got the hots for your Billy!

Claire   No I haven't! I haven't at all!

Fan (*shouts*)   Don't let him push you off the ball! Push him back! It's a man's game, y'know!

Billy   Moz! Come on!

Elaine   Hey, Stevie Mac. You and him should come down the park some time. If you're allowed to stop runnin' for a minute.

Moz   I'm allowed to do whatever I want.

Elaine   Oh yeah?

Moz   Comin' down the park some time, Billy?

Billy *looks over at them, but isn't sure what to say, so he just keeps running, jumping, running, turning, running, jumping, running, turning.*

Elaine   He's scared. Aw, look, he's scared.

Moz   I'm not scared.

Claire   There's nothin' to be scared of, Billy. I'll look after yer.

Billy *loses his concentration for a moment and the* **Liverpool Midfielder** *steals in and volleys the ball high up into the air.*

Commentator   Walters lost a bit of concentration there! Not a great clearance, though . . .

As the **Liverpool Full Back** *and the* **Everton Striker** *prepare to challenge for it, and the* **Referee** *pays close attention,* **Billy** *leaps even higher than before, straining every sinew to win the header, and becomes:*

Nine   EVERTON 0 − LIVERPOOL 0

Billy, *aged fourteen, climbing a* **Tree** *in the park.*

Claire   Billy, come down!

Billy   Yer can see all the pitches in one go from the top of 'ere! Looks amazin'!

Claire   Billy!

Billy   You come up!

Claire   I can't climb trees, can I?!

Billy   I can. I'm great at climbin' trees. Aren't I ace at climbin' trees, Claire?

Claire   I like yer coat, Billy. It's lovely and warm and it . . .

Billy   What?

Claire   Smells of yer.

Billy   In a bad way?

Claire   No. A good way. A nice smell.

Billy   Oh, right. Right. (*Beat.*) Eh, feels like I'm a commentator. Y'know? Up in the stand. (*Beat.*) You've gotta come up. I need a summariser . . .

Claire   I ain't got the right shoes on.

Billy *puts his hand to his mouth like a microphone.*

Billy   'And here she is, makin' her debut as Billy Walters' girlfriend – Claire Gibson!'

Claire   Stupid!

Billy   'There are big things expected of Miss Gibson and she's already a fans' favourite!'

Billy *makes the sound of* **Fans** *cheering.*

Claire   Stop it, Billy!

Billy *and* **Claire** *laugh.*

Tree (*sings*)
  Billy and Claire, up a tree, K.I.S.S.I.N.G.
  Billy and Claire, up a tree, K.I.S.S.I.N.G.

Claire   Can't wait for Friday. We'll have such a laugh.

Billy   Friday?

Claire   Pleasureland!

Billy   I . . . I won't be able to go on Friday.

Claire   You said yer would.

Billy   I didn't know yer meant on Friday.

Claire   Everyone's goin'.

Billy   I've got trainin' on Friday.

Claire   Yer can miss one.

Billy   I can't.

Claire   Moz is goin' with Elaine.

Billy   Why don't you come up, eh? The view's boss.

Claire   I will.

Billy   Smart!

Claire   If you come on Friday.

Billy   Claire . . .

Claire   Billy, it ain't just the rides and that – I don't even like the rides, I don't feel safe – it's the candyfloss and stuff like that. The balloons! Not normal balloons, the floaty balloons, y'know. Balloons where you have to hold the string dead tight or they'll be up and away. I love all that. (*Beat.*) Come on, Billy, eh?

Queen Jean (*sings*)
　The whole thing's daft, I don't know why
　You have to laugh, or else you cry.

Claire   Billy?

Queen Jean (*sings*)
　You have to live or else you die
　You have to laugh or else you cry.

Billy   I can't, Claire. Sorry.

Claire (*beat*)   I could ask 'em if they wanna swap it to Saturday. What d'yer reckon?

Billy   Claire –

Claire   What?

Billy   Saturday, I play. I can't do Saturday.

Claire   You can't do Fridays, you can't do Saturdays – what can you do?

Billy   Well, not Mondays or Wednesdays, but . . . I . . . I can do the rest.

Claire   I'm gonna go and look for the others.

Billy   Don't. Come up, eh?

Claire *shakes her head and backs away.* **Billy** *looks up at the sky, then stretches his neck towards it, closes his eyes and heads the ball powerfully, before falling back to the ground.*

Liverpool Full Back   Climbin'! He was climbin, Ref!

Commentator   Walters was brave there! He could have hurt himself.

Summariser   Towering header! Great leap for a little man!

Billy *scrambles back to his feet and becomes:*

Ten   EVERTON 0 – LIVERPOOL 0

Billy, *aged fifteen, approaching* **Bill Sr** *at the Pier Head. As he does so, two* **Sailors** *and a* **Shantyman** *appear, singing and going about their business.*

Shantyman (*sings*)
  I'll sing you a song, a good song of the sea

Sailors (*respond*)
  With a way, hey, blow the man down

Shantyman (*sings*)
  And trust that you'll join in the chorus with me

Sailors (*respond*)
  Give me some time to blow the man down.

Billy   Dad! Me and Auntie Mo've been lookin' everywhere for yer.

Bill Sr   Well, you've found me.

Billy   D'yer know what time it is?

Bill Sr   Does it matter?

Billy   Have yer had loads to drink?

Bill Sr   Not nearly enough.

Billy   You coulda rung, y'know.

Bill Sr   I didn't think anyone'd notice.

Billy   Yeah, well, I noticed, didn't I? And Mo. She'd brought us pasties round and everythin'.

Bill Sr (*beat*)   I like how the moon's on the water. How it looks like it is. Like you could just swim the moon.

Billy   Come 'ed, eh, she's in the car.

Bill Sr *doesn't move.*

Shantyman (*sings*)
  There was an old skipper, I don't know his name

Sailors (*respond*)
With a way, hey, blow the man down

Shantyman (*sings*)
And though he once played a remarkable game

Sailors (*respond*)
Give me some time to blow the man down.

Bill Sr   When your grandad worked 'ere this was a different world, y'know. You wouldn't believe how many ships there used to be. How many people. Loadin' and unloadin' and sailin' off to all four corners. You just wouldn't believe.

Billy   Dad, it's freezin'. Can we go?

Bill Sr   One thing they unloaded was the tunes, y'know, mate. The sailors went the game and sung their work songs at play. And when they sailed away, the songs stayed. Y'know, and chants and that. This city's where it all started. This is its home. And that game was loaded back onto the ships, and taken all round the world . . .

Shantyman (*sings*)
His ship lay becalmed on the tropical sea

Sailors (*respond*)
With a way, hey, blow the man down

Shantyman (*sings*)
He whistled all day but in vain for a breeze

Sailors (*respond*)
Give me some time to blow the man down.

Bill Sr   What do I do? (*Shouts.*) What am I meant to do?

Billy   Are yer . . . talkin' to me? (*Beat.*) I . . . I bet there's a game on the box. Bet there is. We could watch it when we get home. We could. Could watch it. Together. Or –

Bill Sr   Shut up, Billy.

Billy   Oh right, is it? Is it? Piss off then!

Bill Sr   I tried to, didn't I! I tried to, but evidently me sister and me son launched a nationwide manhunt the moment a flamin' pasty went cold!

Billy   OK then. Fine. Stay here!

Bill Sr   I will, thanks!

Billy   See ya!

Bill Sr   So long!

Pause.

Billy   I'll leave yer me windcheater . . .

The **Liverpool Full Back** *dwells on the ball for a moment, but* **Billy** *doesn't tackle him. Instead he waits for him to pass it, then chases after the* **Liverpool Midfielder** *and pulls his shirt back. The* **Referee** *blows his whistle.*

Billy   Never!

Referee   Pulling!

Billy   He was pullin' me!

The **Referee** *blows his whistle again and summons* **Billy** *over to him. As* **Billy** *marches over, he becomes:*

Eleven   EVERTON 0 − LIVERPOOL 0

Billy, *aged sixteen, standing opposite* **Moz** *in the attic of Auntie Mo's house. Between them are two bars with table-footballers on.* **Moz** *is holding one of the bars.* **Billy** *clutches some five-pound notes in his hand and stares at them with wonder.*

Moz   Billy, it's thirty-five quid. What's amazin' about thirty-five quid? Just play, will yer . . . ?

Billy   It's not thirty-five quid. It's so much more than that.

Moz   How much is it then?

Billy   It's gettin' paid . . . for football. For playin' football.
Every day. That's like gettin' paid . . . for breathin'.

Billy *spins the other bar.* **Moz** *lets go of his bar, and lifts up his shirt.*
He is wearing a tool-belt round his waist. He pulls a screwdriver from it.

Moz   Not bein' funny, mate, but see this? This means I'll get
loads more than that. This means I'll be able to treat Elaine
like a princess. Means it don't matter even a tiny bit that me
al' fellah's gone, cos I'll be able to help me mam out more than
he ever did. Sparkies can rake it in! The world is in need of
illumination! And this is the key to everythin' . . .

Billy   But *this* . . . is *football*.

Billy *spins his bar again.*

Moz   You spun again. You're not allowed to spin. You're
always spinnin', you!

Billy   D'yer remember when I got me first footie? On me
birthday. D'yer remember what it said in me card?

Moz   Yeah. I do.

Billy   I *will* score the winner in the derby. You watch!

Moz   Billy . . .

Billy   What?

Fan (*shouts*)   Now! Yes! Now! Have a go!

Moz *grips the screwdriver in his hand tightly.*

Moz   I like bein' a fan. (*Beat.*) I like other people breathin' in
when I do. I like shoutin' and not bein' able to hear the shout
cos everyone else is shoutin' too. I like my heart going boom . . .

Billy   Well, duh – yer can get paid and still be a fan, divvy.

Moz   No, Billy, I don't think you can.

Billy   Course.

Moz   Bein' a fan costs money. Never ever makes it. Always
ends up down. Moment you're up, that's it.

Billy   That's rubbish.

Moz   Moment you're up, the fan's –

Billy   What?

Moz   Dead, Billy. And buried.

Moz *puts the screwdriver back into his tool-belt, and then – as* **Billy** *stares at his cash – he spins the bar.*

Moz   Get in!

Billy   That is rubbish, Ref!

Referee   Excuse me, lad. You're not in the stand now, y'know. Address the match official with respect, please.

Billy   Oh, but come –

Referee   I mean it, Walters.

Liverpool Midfielder   Book him, Ref!

Billy *pushes the* **Liverpool Midfielder**, *who pushes him back. As the* **Referee** *blows his whistle, and the* **Liverpool Full Back** *tries to come between them,* **Billy** *becomes:*

Twelve   EVERTON 0 – LIVERPOOL 0

Billy, *still aged sixteen, in a city-centre hotel with his* **Agent** *and* **Bill Sr**.

Agent   Five star, Billy boy. Ever been in a five-star hotel before?

Billy *shakes his head.* **Bill Sr** *doesn't respond.*

Agent   And where did the other fellah take you?

Billy   Travelodge. On the Lancs.

Bill Sr   I don't really see what that's gotta do with anythin'.

Agent   And the free boots? The free shinnies?

Billy *shakes his head again.*

Bill Sr He's already got boots and shinnies.

Agent Bill, Bill, Bill. It's OK. You're looking out for your boy, I know that. Well, rest assured, he can trust his Uncle Paul. You both can. Uncle Paul is in it for the long haul.

Fans (*sing*)
  We'll support you
  We'll support you
  We'll support you evermore!

Agent You've got fire in your belly, Billy, and so have I. You need proper representation. You need guidance.

Bill Sr We'll take a bit o' time to think about it if that's OK.

Agent The sun is coming up on me and you, Billy boy. The free boots? The free shinnies? The five-star hang-out? This is just the beginning. I'll see you right, Billy. You really can trust your Uncle Paul.

The **Agent** *offers his hand to* **Billy**.

Bill Sr Billy, why don't we –

Billy *shakes the* **Agent**'s *hand, then the* **Referee** *speaks:*

Referee Right, now get on with the game . . .

The **Liverpool Full Back** *takes a quick free kick to the* **Liverpool Midfielder**, *but* **Billy** *whips it off his toes, then drags it back, leaves them both for dead, and sprints away with the ball.*

Summariser Oh, audacious piece of skill there!

Fans (*sing*)
  You are my Everton, my only Everton
  You make me happy
  When skies are grey
  You never noticed
  How much I love you
  So please don't take
  My Everton away
  Nah-nah-nah-nah-nah.

As the **Fans** *sing,* **Billy** *becomes:*

Thirteen EVERTON 0 − LIVERPOOL 0

Billy, *aged seventeen, doing dribbling drills in training with the youth team at Netherton. The* **Everton Boss** *watches alongside the* **Youth Coach**.

Everton Boss Walters! A word!

Billy *stops dribbling, and jogs over apprehensively.*

Everton Boss Dave tells me you've been one of his strongest players this year.

Billy I've done OK, boss.

Everton Boss Keep it up, lad, and we'll get you over to Bellefield, eh? See what you're like against the big boys.

Billy *nods, and is clearly keen to start dribbling again.*

Everton Boss Go on then . . .

Billy *grins and heads back to the drill.*

Everton Boss And always play like your life depends upon it!

Billy *gets back on the ball, and does exactly that . . .*

Fans (*sing*)
    Oh we hate Bill Shankly and we hate St John
    But most of all we hate Big Ron
    And we'll hang the Kopites one by one
    On the banks of the royal-blue Mersey
    And so to hell with Liverpool and Rangers too
    We'll throw them all in the Mersey
    And we'll fight fight fight with all our might
    For the boys in the royal-blue jerseys!

Billy *performs a Cruyff-turn and bears down on the* **Liverpool Full Back** *and the* **Liverpool Midfielder** *once more. The* **Everton Striker** *finds space.*

Commentator Some run by Walters. Really opening up for him here. And Liverpool are outnumbered . . .

Billy *performs step-over after step-over in front of the* **Liverpool Midfielder** *and becomes:*

Fourteen   EVERTON 0 − LIVERPOOL 0

Billy, *still aged seventeen, clutching his football and faced by his* **Agent** *in a city-centre hotel.*

Agent   I told 'em Real Madrid had enquired about you. Barcelona too.

Billy   D'you think that's true?

Agent   I said to them − this kid's the Next Big Thing. You know it, and I know it.

Billy   Have they given me a contract then?

Agent (*laughs*)   Have they given . . . ?

Billy   Have they?

Commentator   Everton have a man free!

Summariser   He's completely unmarked in the middle!

Agent   Best not to carry that tatty football around with you any more, eh, Billy, I mean, think of the −

Billy   Paul. What have I got?

Agent   Four.

Billy   Four years?

Agent   At six.

Billy   Six hundred quid a week? Four years at six hundred quid a week? Right. Right. Right.

Billy *feints to go one way, then the other, but the* **Liverpool Midfielder** *reads it and nips the ball away from him.*

Commentator   He's lost it!

Summariser   It's broken for them though! The striker's lining one up! He's gonna try one!

The **Everton Striker** *pulls his leg back and everything slows down.*

Liverpool Midfielder   Billy?

Billy   What?

Agent   Billy boy?

Billy   What, Paul?

The **Everton Striker** *shoots and the action freezes.*

Agent   Six grand.

Billy   Eh?

Agent   Not six hundred. Six . . . thousand.

Billy's *jaw drops and the action instantly returns to normal.*

Commentator   It's there!

As the ball hits the back of the net, the **Crowd** *goes wild.* **Billy** *sinks to his knees, drops his football and clenches his fists, the* **Everton Striker** *punches the air, the* **Referee** *returns to the centre circle, and the* **Liverpool Full Back** *argues with the* **Liverpool Midfielder**.

Commentator   What a finish! Just when it looked like young Walters had overplayed it. And in the thirty-eighth minute of the Merseyside derby it's Everton, one – Liverpool, nil! (*Beat.*) Let's look at the replay . . .

Agent   Billy boy?

Billy   What, Paul?

Agent   Six grand.

Billy   Eh?

Agent   Not six hundred. Six . . . thousand.

Commentator   And one more time . . .

Billy   Eh?

Agent   Not six hundred. Six . . . thousand.

As the ball hits the back of the net again, the **Crowd** *goes wild,* **Billy** *sinks to his knees, drops his football and clenches his fists, and the* **Everton Striker** *punches the air once more.*

Commentator   And that's relieved the pressure on the Everton Boss!

Summariser   Temporarily at least . . .

Billy *high-fives the* **Everton Boss***.*

Fans (*sing*)
  And it's Everton, Everton FC
  We're by far the greatest team
  The world has ever seen!

The **Liverpool Midfielder** *and the* **Liverpool Full Back** *restart the action, but the* **Everton Striker** *immediately steals possession back and sprays the ball out wide to* **Billy***.* **Billy** *leaps and takes it on his chest. As the* **Liverpool Full Back** *approaches him,* **Billy** *doesn't move – just stands there with his hands on his hips and becomes:*

Fifteen   EVERTON 1 – LIVERPOOL 0

Billy*, aged eighteen, in the living room of the Walters' flat, with a holdall over his shoulder, a plastic bag in one hand and a copy of* Roy of the Rovers *in the other.*

Bill Sr   Alright, mate. Goin' out?

Billy   Movin' out.

Commentator   Well, would you look at that?

Summariser   The arrogance of youth!

Billy   Paul's sorted me with a place down the dock.

Bill Sr   You've got a place. Our place. Here.

Billy   This is a good investment.

Bill Sr   This is home.

Billy   I'm not a kid any more.

Bill Sr   You're only eighteen.

Billy   I need my own space.

Bill Sr   You've got your room.

Billy   You don't understand.

Bill Sr   What don't I understand?

Billy   It's embarrassin'!

Bill Sr   What is?

Billy   They've all got penthouses and big detached numbers and I've got . . . the same box room in the same high-rise I've been in since I was eight years old.

Fans (*sing*)
    What's it like to be outclassed?

Bill Sr   You'll still come round, won't yer?

Billy   When I get chance.

Bill Sr   Can I come round to yours?

Billy   Ring first.

Bill Sr   When are you gonna get the rest of your stuff?

Billy   I've got all the stuff I want.

Bill Sr   You'll need more stuff than that.

Billy   I'll get new stuff.

Bill Sr   Billy . . .

Billy   What?

Bill Sr   This'll *always* be home, y'know.

As the **Liverpool Full Back** *lunges at the ball,* **Billy** *nutmegs him –
but just runs it out of play. The* **Everton Boss** *claps his hands.*

Everton Boss   Brilliant, Billy! Brilliant!

Around the ground, a new chant starts to the tune of 'Tom Hark':

Fans (*sing*)
   Billy Walters, Billy Walters
   Billy Walters, Billy Walters
   Billy Walters, Billy Walters
   Billy Walters, Billy Walters

As **Billy** *spins round and takes it in, he becomes:*

Sixteen   EVERTON 1 — LIVERPOOL 0

Billy, *aged nineteen, in the manager's office at Bellefield. He is staring at the pictures on the wall as the* **Everton Boss** *enters.*

Everton Boss   Look at those pictures. The Cannonball Kid. The Golden Vision. Ball. Latchford. Andy Gray when he was a hero, not a gobshite. Great players. Great players.

Billy   I've not done anythin' wrong have I, boss?

Everton Boss   No, Billy. No. You've been doin' a lot o' things right. Y'know we've got a few injury problems for the derby? And I'm under a bit o' pressure at the moment.

Billy   Nah.

Everton Boss   Trust me. I am.

Billy   Right.

Everton Boss   I gave you that contract cos I believe in you. I've always seen you as one for the future. (*Beat.*) Billy?

Billy   Boss?

Everton Boss   The future starts now. I'm choosing you. For the bench.

Fan (*shouts*)   That's it, boys! That's it! Get it down on the deck! Come on! Play 'em off the park!

Everton Boss   If you have a word with Jeanette on your way out, she'll sort out tickets for your family. OK?

Billy   Oh, nah, that's alright, boss, jus' . . . jus' one for me agent. Just one for Paul. That's all.

Everton Boss   Sure?

Billy (*beat*)   Yeah.

Everton Boss   It's your dream to play in the derby, innit, lad?

Billy   No, boss. To *score* in the derby.

The **Everton Boss** *grins.*

Everton Boss   Well, if you do that, I'll stick your picture up there alongside them, OK? And Billy?

Billy   What, gaffer?

Everton Boss   If you get on . . .

Billy   Yeah?

Everton Boss   Put your heart and soul into it. Heart. And soul.

Billy *nods and the* **Fourth Official** *holds up a board with a number 3 on it.*

Commentator   And the Fourth Official's indicating that they'll be three minutes added on to this half. Can the Reds get back into it before the break?

With the action down the other end, **Billy** *stands alone on the halfway line.*

Billy (*shouts*)   Clear it! Hit it long! I'm free! I'm in space!

The ball runs loose and the **Everton Striker** *boots it long downfield, then tries to catch* **Billy** *up . . .*

Everton Striker   And again, Billy! I'm with yer!

Commentator   Chance of a break here . . .

Summariser   If the lad can control it −

Commentator   He could be clean through!

As **Billy** *watches the ball, he becomes:*

Seventeen   EVERTON I − LIVERPOOL O

Billy, *still aged nineteen, getting the final brief instructions from the* **Everton Boss** *before coming on earlier in the game.*

Everton Boss   Stay on that wing and get chalk on your boots. Run at 'em. Scare 'em. And don't let it pass you by . . .

Billy *nods, takes a deep breath, then turns and controls the ball perfectly with his instep before running through on goal.*

Commentator   He is, y'know! He's through!

Everton Striker   Billy! Square!

Commentator   And he's got support!

Summariser   I don't think he'll need him! I think he's got the confidence to go it alone!

Commentator   This could be two for Everton!

As **Billy** *races towards the goal, the* **Crowd** *breathes in, everything starts to slow down, and moments appear around him.*

Everton Boss   The future starts now.

Bill Sr   This'll *always* be home, y'know.

Agent   Not six hundred. Six . . . thousand.

Moz   Bein' a fan costs money. Never ever makes it. Always ends up down.

Bill Sr   I like how the moon's on the water. How it looks like it is. Like you could just swim the moon.

Claire   It's the candyfloss and stuff like that. The balloons!

Elaine   Claire's got the hots for your Billy!

Bill Sr   'Wonderful', Billy! 'Wonderful'!

Moz   Can't beat me! Can't beat me!

Queen Jean   You can be a star, y'know. It'll be like it was with Latchford. It'll be painted on the walls of Walton. Billy Walters Walks on Water. Billy Walters Walks on Water. You can do it, Billy. You can. One day you'll score the winner in the derby.

Shiner   What d'you wanna be, Billy?

Clifford   Yeah, what d'you wanna be?

Bill Sr   I can't just click my fingers and make everythin' better, y'know. I wish I could, but I can't.

Billy *closes his eyes and shoots . . .*

Queen Jean (*sings*)
   We're heading for disaster, but I just don't care
   Shut your eyes and count to ten, you won't be there.

Bill Sr   This *is* home.

All   Awwwwwhhhh!!!

Commentator   He's missed it! He's hit it over!

Summariser   Took his eye off the ball!

Billy *drops to his knees, puts his head in his hands, the* **Crowd** *breathes out, and everything returns to normal.*

Fans (*chant*)
   Who are yer
   Who are yer
   Who are yer?

As the **Fans** *chant,* **Billy** *becomes:*

Eighteen   EVERTON I — LIVERPOOL O

Billy, *aged thirty, crouching opposite* **Bill Sr** *in the living room of the Walters' flat with the* **Subbuteo Footballers** *between them.*

Billy   If I'd've just –

Bill Sr   Forget it, Billy.

Commentator   Oh, I hope the boy doesn't live to regret that one . . .

Billy   But if I . . . if I could've . . . if I'd –

Bill Sr   Billy . . .

The **Subbuteo Referee** *blows his whistle.*

Half-Time

Around the performance space, refreshments and merchandise continue to be sold while the **Bookie** *is clearly dispirited.*

Bookie   Everton win, five to one on. Can't do better than that. Gotta clothe the kids. Gotta feed the missus. Billy Walters, young Billy Walters, now eight to one the winner. Anyone who got thirty-threes . . . you shoulda worn a mask.

As the crowd re-enters the performance space, the **MC** *appears on the pitch once more.*

MC   And if you'd like to check your ticket, ladies and gents, the golden goal time today is forty-one minutes and eighteen seconds. If that's you, could you please make yourself known to the nearest available steward? We'll have you on the pitch at the next home game for the hit-the-bar competition when you too will have the opportunity to win a Ford Fiesta – with only two previous owners – courtesy of our friends and yours, Nev's Nearly-New Motors of Aigburth. Thank you.

When the stands are full, 'It's Enough to Make Your Heart Go' starts to play.

Ladies and gentleman, here come the teams again – so please let's hear it for . . . Everton . . . and . . . Liverpool!

Second Half

One   EVERTON 1 – LIVERPOOL 0

Billy, *aged thirty, crouches opposite* **Bill Sr**, *in the living room of the Walters' flat.* **Subbuteo Footballers** *are in between them. As the* **Subbuteo Referee** *blows his whistle, the* **Crowd** *roars once more and* **Billy** *and* **Bill Sr** *flick their* **Subbuteo Footballers**, *who – along with the* **Subbuteo Referee** *– immediately leap from their bases and charge after the ball again.*

Bill Sr   I'm gonna start tryin' now, Billy!

Billy   Oh eh, listen to it, will yer!

Bill Sr   The gloves are comin' off now, mate, I'm serious. No more Mr Nice Guy!

Billy   Alright then, Mouth, let's have ya!

Billy *and the* **Liverpool Full Back** *challenge for the ball. The ball runs loose to the* **Everton Striker** *who immediately draws the* **Liverpool Midfielder** *and knocks it into space for* **Billy** *to run onto . . .*

Commentator   And we're back under way, folks! One–nil to the Blues at the break, but could so easily have been two. There's more goals in this game, that's for sure. Everything to play for, so hold on to your bob hats, everybody – this could be one to remember!

Billy *takes the ball in his stride, then knocks it past the* **Liverpool Full Back** *and tries to beat him for pace.*

Commentator   And Walters is picking up where he left off! One for him to chase and just look at his pace!

As **Billy** *gets to the ball, the* **Liverpool Full Back** *dives in and clips his back leg.* **Billy** *spins round, trying to stay upright, and becomes:*

Two   EVERTON I − LIVERPOOL O

Billy, *aged nineteen, alone in the dressing room an hour after the derby match. His leg is stretched out in front of him.* **Bill Sr** *enters. He is clearly intimidated by his surroundings and clutches a copy of the* Football Pink.

Billy   What are you doin' 'ere?

Bill Sr   Me and your Auntie Mo and Maurice was watchin' it on the telly, and then . . . when you came on . . . I couldn't watch any more. How ridiculous is that? So I came 'ere. *Had to.* Been stood outside the ground for two hours. In the street. Just . . . listenin'.

Billy   You can't just walk into the dressin' room, y'know. The physio'll be back in a minute.

Bill Sr   Billy, have yer not heard?

Billy   What?

Bill Sr   Your boss has just quit. That's what everyone's sayin'.

Commentator   That's knocked the young lad off his stride! Can he stay on his feet?

Billy   Maybe he should've picked me earlier then, eh?

Pause.

Bill Sr   I didn't know you'd got injured. Was waitin' for yer. And then when I seen all the others head off, I asked the bloke on the door. And get this: when I said who I was he held the door open for me. Led me down the corridor like a VIP! S'pose that means you're not Bill Walters' lad any more. S'pose that means I'm Billy Walters' dad.

Billy   You shouldn't be in 'ere.

Bill Sr   Is your knee alright?

Billy   Two weeks tops. They're gonna take me for a scan, but it's fine.

Bill Sr   Yeah?

Billy   Yeah.

Bill Sr   Billy, you got an eight.

Billy   A what?

Bill Sr   Out o' ten. In the *Pink*. I only ever used to get sixes. Always sixes. You got an eight. On your debut. In the derby.

Billy   Right.

Bill Sr *hands* **Billy** *the* Football Pink. **Billy** *glances at it.*

Bill Sr   I heard them chant your name. I heard it. I'm stood there, no one around, and it hits me like a ball in the face. What a game. What a game. (*Beat.*) I'm thinkin' I'm . . . I'm gonna start . . . coachin'. Just kids and that like, but – I mean eh, I might be shite – but . . . give it a go, y'know. I'd like to. I would. I'd like to.

Billy   You'd better go.

Fan (*shouts*)   Now! Now! Move it! Now!

Bill Sr   Come round ours. For your tea. I don't mean today, I've got not'in in, but tomorrow, tomorrow, yeah. You could, mate. I'll go to Marksies and get a couple o' those fancy ones. They're good. They're a treat. I'll get afters 'n' everythin'. Tomorrow then?

Billy   I can't tomorrow. I'm buyin' a car.

Bill Sr   What's wrong with your old one?

Billy   Not'in.

Bill Sr   Well, why yer gettin' a newie?

Billy   I need two.

Bill Sr   Yer don't *need*, do yer?

Billy   I do, yeah.

Bill Sr   Yer mean yer *want*.

Billy   Same thing.

Bill Sr   Isn't.

Billy   OK.

Bill Sr   Billy, you're nineteen, you live in a city-centre flat –

Billy   Apartment! It's an apartment! You live in a flat! I live in an apartment!

Bill Sr   There is no reason for you to have two cars. Since when did I ever have two cars?

Billy   Yeah, but . . .

Bill Sr   What?

Billy   You were a six, weren't yer? And me? I'm an eight.

Billy *holds the* Football Pink *out for* **Bill Sr** *and, as he takes it,* **Billy** *spins round again and hits the deck heavily.*

Commentator   Could be a booking, that one . . .

Summariser   He barely touched him!

The **Referee** *blows his whistle and, while the* **Liverpool Full Back** *pleads his innocence,* **Billy** *thrusts his arm in the air and indicates he needs treatment.*

Fans (*sing*)
Your're goin' home in a St John's Ambulance
Woh-oh-oh!

As the **Referee** *leans over him,* **Billy** *becomes:*

Three   EVERTON I – LIVERPOOL 0

Billy, *aged twenty, lying in a hospital bed in a private room.* **Moz** *is alongside him.*

Moz   I can't stay long, Billy. I've got a job booked in.

Billy   You've only jus' got 'ere.

Moz   Eh, I've got you somethin' though!

Moz *pulls a copy of* Roy of the Rovers *out of his back pocket and offers it to* **Billy**. **Billy** *takes the comic and stares at it. Pause.*

Moz   I could get me mam to pop in later if yer want. If I tell her they've got UK Gold in 'ere, she'll stay for hours!

Billy   What about me dad?

Moz   He said to do everythin' they tell you to do.

Billy   Why couldn't he tell me that himself?

Moz   Y'know he hates hospitals.

Billy   Oh yeah, and everyone else loves 'em. We all think they're ace, don't we?

Moz   Come on, Billy. You'll be out in a couple o' days.

Billy   It's rubbish in 'ere.

Billy *pushes the comic away from him.*

Moz   Nobody wants to have an operation, do they, Billy, but yer can't get through a career without one. With a bit o' luck, this'll sort it . . .

Billy   Forget the job, Moz.

Moz   What?

Billy   Come and work for me.

Moz   Why would you need an electrician workin' for yer?

Billy   Not as a sparky, as a PA. Few o' the lads've got 'em. Bein' a footballer's not just about football any more, y'know. I am in need of assistance. You could develop Brand Billy!

Moz   Brand Billy?

Billy   I'll pay you more than you're on.

Moz   No, Billy, nah – I mean, think what Elaine'd say.

Billy   I'm not askin' Elaine. I'm askin' you.

Moz   Billy, I –

Billy   Isn't there just a bit of you that thinks 'What if?' What if you'd kept playin'? What if you'd never met Elaine? What if you'd never swapped a footie for a screwdriver? Come and live my life, Moz. Come and live it with me.

Fans (*chant*)
   Cheat cheat cheat cheat!

Moz *shakes his head, but* **Billy** *immediately starts trying to get up.*

Billy   Give us an 'and, mate. You can start by assistin' us to the pub across the road.

Moz   Billy, I said no.

Billy   I've had enough o' this room.

Moz   I've got a job booked in.

Billy   I want a pint.

Moz   You can't have one.

Billy   I'm a flare player, Maurice! A winger! A maverick! I do the unexpected. I do what others don't. That, my friend, is what makes me me!

Moz   You're crackers you, Billy Walters!

Billy   Come 'ed, O'Connor la'!

Moz *pulls* **Billy** *up, while the* **Physio** *passes* **Billy** *a water bottle and wipes his face with the magic sponge. The* **Referee** *turns and books the* **Liverpool Full Back***.*

Commentator   Walters is alright. The magic sponge has done the trick! It's a yellow for the Liverpool full back, though. Bit harsh that and the crowd aren't happy. It's turned the volume up in here alright!

Billy *takes a swig from the bottle, then throws it off the pitch and becomes:*

Four   EVERTON 1 − LIVERPOOL 0

Billy, *aged twenty-one, sitting in the tactics room at Bellefield. The* **New Boss** *hands the* **Players** *team sheets, then pushes counters round a mock-up of a pitch.*

New Boss   This is the team for Saturday. I'm going to go with a five-three-two − giving the wing backs plenty of licence to get forward.

The **Players** *all focus on the counters, apart from* **Billy** *who continues to study the team sheet.*

New Boss   We're going to sit two in midfield to shield the back three, and play one in the hole behind the front two to disrupt the flow from their −

Billy   I'm not in this.

New Boss   Sorry?

Billy   I'm not in this team.

New Boss   Anybody who wants to talk to me individually can talk to me afterwards. (*Beat.*) By playing this way, we'll −

Billy   I'm not even on the bench.

New Boss   Did you hear what I just said?

Billy   I mean, I'm not bein' funny but who in this team's gonna get the fans on their feet?

New Boss   I'm talking, William!

Billy   But I'm fit!

New Boss   D'you want to leave the room?

Billy   I'm not a kid.

New Boss   Then don't act like one. This sort of behaviour might've been acceptable under the previous management, but I'm the boss now. OK?

Billy *shakes his head moodily.*

New Boss   Do you understand? (*Beat.*) Do . . . you . . . under . . . stand?

Billy (*quietly*)   Yeah.

New Boss   Pardon?

Billy   Yes.

New Boss   Good.

Billy's *head sinks.*

Fans (*sing*)
    Don't be mistaken and don't be misled
    You're not really Scousers
    You're from Birkenhead
    Where's your Cathedral
    And where's your Pier Head
    In your sheep-shaggin' home?

The **Everton Boss** *claps his hands together.*

Everton Boss   Wake up, Billy! Come on!

Everton Striker   Yours, Billy!

The **Everton Striker** *passes the ball to* **Billy**, *but his path is immediately blocked by the* **Liverpool Full Back**. **Billy** *turns the other way, but the* **Liverpool Midfielder** *is lying in wait.*

Commentator   Walters is under pressure here!

Summariser   Where's he going?

He dribbles back towards his own goal, desperately looking for an escape, until the pair muscle him out of possession.

Commentator   And he's lost it! He's lost it!

Everton Striker   Billy!

Billy   Referee! Referee! All over me!

Referee   Play on!

As the **Liverpool Midfielder** *and the* **Liverpool Full Back** *break forward,* **Billy** *holds his arms out in frustration and becomes:*

Five   EVERTON I — LIVERPOOL O

Billy, *still aged twenty-one, standing alone in the manager's office at Bellefield. As the* **Liverpool Midfielder** *and the* **Liverpool Full Back** *continue their attack, the action slows down. The* **New Boss** *enters.*

New Boss   You know why you're here, don't you, William?

Billy   The contract?

New Boss   That's right.

Billy   You're prob'ly best talkin' to Paul, mate.

New Boss   I'm not your mate, William. I'm your boss.

Billy   Paul deals with all that, though, boss. He's the man to negotiate with.

New Boss   Yeah. I know.

Billy   You've got rid of the players.

New Boss   Pardon?

Billy   On the wall. The old boss used to have pictures of great players up.

New Boss   There's no such thing as great players, son. Only great teams.

Billy *pulls a face. The* **Liverpool Midfielder** *plays a defence-splitting pass through for the* **Liverpool Full Back**.

Commentator   Oh, and there could be a chance here, y'know!

New Boss   I think the club was irresponsible giving you a four-year deal. I think you still had everything to prove.

Billy   But I did though, didn't I? I proved it.

New Boss   You didn't prove anything at all.

Billy   What about the derby?

New Boss   One match? Two years ago?

Billy   I've had bad luck.

New Boss   Mm.

Billy   The knee's gettin' there now, though. Just takes time.

New Boss   It's not just the knee, is it?

Billy *looks at the* **Liverpool Midfielder** *as he runs through on goal.*

Summariser   Has he got the finish?!

Billy   Get a bit bored, boss, to tell ya the truth. Y'know when I . . . can't play, or I'm not playin' as well as I can. Get a bit . . . frustrated.

New Boss   Which player doesn't?

Billy   You've not had to fine me for a few weeks though, have yer? Eh? Been on my b-b-best behaviour.

New Boss   William . . .

Billy   Yeah?

As the **Liverpool Full Back** *pulls his leg back to shoot* – *the action freezes.*

New Boss   We're not going to be renewing your contract. Obviously.

Billy (*beat*)   Obviously?

New Boss   Obviously. I realise it's disappointing news. I understand, believe me. We've all had disappointments. But use this as a wake-up call. Get the hunger back. Start trying to be a footballer on the pitch again, rather than just off it, eh, William?

Billy   It's Billy!

New Boss (*beat*)   If I'm absolutely honest, I've never been convinced that you're as good as you think you are.

Billy   And who are you, eh? You were rubbish!

New Boss   Maybe you're right – but what little bit I had I squeezed every last drop out of. And here I am. Where will you be a few years down the line?

Billy   Wherever I wanna be, mate.

New Boss   I'm not your mate.

Billy   You're not my boss.

New Boss   You're right, William. I'm not.

Commentator (*shouts*)   It's in!

Summariser (*shouts*)   What a shot!

There is a roar from the **Crowd** *and the action returns to normal as the* **Liverpool Midfielder** *and the* **Liverpool Full Back** *both drop to their knees and punch the air, and* **Billy** *chases after the* **Referee**.

Billy   They were pullin'! They were pushin'! Was a foul! Was offside!

Commentator   And let's just look at that through-ball. Was he on?

New Boss   We're not going to be renewing your contract. Obviously.

Billy (*beat*)   Obviously?

New Boss   Obviously.

Summariser   He was level. There has to be daylight. And what about that finish, eh?

Billy   You're not my boss.

New Boss   You're right, William. I'm not.

Once more, the **Crowd** *roars, and the* **Liverpool Midfielder** *and the* **Liverpool Full Back** *drop to their knees and punch the air.*

Commentator   And it's Everton, one – Liverpool, one! Game on!

Fans (*sing*)
    Oh . . . I am a Liverpudlian
    I come from the Spion Kop
    I like to sing, I like to shout
    I go there quite a lot (every week)

> We've won the League, we've won the cup
> We've been to Europe too
> We played the Toffees for a laugh
> And we left them feeling blue
> One—one!

In the centre circle **Billy** *restarts the action with the* **Everton Striker**, *but is immediately under pressure from the* **Liverpool Midfielder**. *As he tries to fend him off, he becomes:*

Six EVERTON I − LIVERPOOL I

Billy, *aged twenty-two, standing in a Travelodge with his* **Agent**.

Agent   I'm a business, Billy boy, not a charity.

Billy   You said you were in it for the long haul.

Agent   I was, I was, but −

Billy   But?

Agent   What more can I do? I've set you up with enough clubs.

Billy   On trial! Why should I have to go on trial? I was man o' the match in the derby!

Agent   Oh, Billy, come on. You know I've tried.

Billy   Tried?

Agent   Yeah.

Billy   This is a Travelodge!

Agent   What's that got to do with anything?

Billy   Real Madrid enquired about me. Barcelona!

Agent   No, they didn't.

Billy   You told me.

Agent   I made that up. To get you a better contract.

Billy   Was in the papers. Must've come from somewhere!

Agent   It did. From me.

Billy   Nah, nah, that ain't right.

Agent   Things change, Billy boy. Everything has an end. This is just ours.

Fans (*sing*)
  Sing when you're winnin'
  You only sing when you're winnin'
  Sing when you're winnin'
  You only sing when you're winnin'!

Billy   Yer said I could trust yer. Said, 'You can trust your Uncle Paul.'

Agent   You could.

Billy   But not now?

Agent   Who can you trust in this world, eh, Billy boy?

Fans (*clap-clap-clap-clap-clap-clap*)   Liv-pool!

Billy *pushes the* **Liverpool Midfielder** *and the* **Referee** *blows his whistle.*

Referee   Push!

Billy   Never!

Referee   You pushed him!

Billy   Kopite . . .

The **Liverpool Midfielder** *chips a quick free kick forward in the direction of the overlapping* **Liverpool Full Back**. *As* **Billy** *chases across, he becomes:*

Seven   EVERTON I − LIVERPOOL I

Billy, *aged twenty-three, standing in his Albert Dock apartment with* **Bill Sr**.

Bill Sr   I'm sure I could find someone who'd let you train with 'em for a couple o' weeks. Y'know, so they could have a good look at yer.

Billy   I don't have to look for a club. Or an agent. They'll come lookin' for me!

Bill Sr   And in the meantime?

Billy   I can do anythin'. Anythin'.

Bill Sr   Well, not anythin', mate.

Billy   What can't I do?

Bill Sr   Billy, you can't even make a cup o' tea . . .

Billy   I can make a cup o' tea!

Bill Sr   You can't, Billy.

Billy   Course I can!

Bill Sr   I'm not bein' funny, I'm jus' sayin'. You need to work out what you're gonna do, that's all. (*Beat.*) I'll make us a cuppa, mate.

Billy   I'll make it . . .

Bill Sr   It's alright . . .

Billy   I can make it!

Bill Sr   OK.

Billy *goes to make a cup of tea.* **Bill Sr** *watches as* **Billy** *hesitates.*

Fans (*sing*)
   Oh, it's all gone quiet over there
   All gone quiet over there
   All gone quiet, all gone quiet
   All gone quiet over there!

Billy *picks up a handful of tea bags and hovers with them.*

Billy   They don't go in the . . . I don't think they, um . . .
I mean, maybe I do it d-d-differently. Maybe everyone else
just . . . just . . . er . . .

Fans   Shhhhh.

Billy *throws down the tea bags and, as the* **Liverpool Full Back**
prepares to head the ball back into the middle, **Billy** *jumps into him. The*
Referee *immediately blows his whistle.*

Billy   What?

Referee   Elbow!

Billy   Rubbish!

The **Referee** *blows his whistle again and motions to* **Billy***. As* **Billy**
walks towards him, he becomes:

Eight   EVERTON 1 — LIVERPOOL 1

Billy*, aged twenty-four, smoking and playing Pro-Evo Football against*
Moz *in the living room of* **Moz** *and* **Elaine***'s house. As he
manoeuvres his gamepad,* **Moz***'s* **Pro-Evo Footballer** *runs round
and performs fancy tricks, but* **Billy***'s* **Pro-Evo Footballer** *pauses.*

Moz   See that? Pure skill!

Billy   Moz?

Moz   Don't try 'n' put me off!

Billy   D'yer think . . . ?

Moz   I'm serious, Billy!

Commentator   The referee might've run out of patience
here. And if he's seen that as an elbow, then Walters could be
off. Could be a straight red.

Billy   Could I move in 'ere with you and Elaine for a bit?

Moz   What?

Billy After I've sold the apartment.

Moz Aw eh, Billy . . .

Billy Just till I find somewhere else.

Moz There's not much room, is there, mate?

Billy I don't take up much space! I'm a winger – I keep to the touchlines!

Moz *stops playing the game. Both* **Pro-Evo Footballers** *pause.*

Moz Billy . . .

Billy Maurice? Mate?

After a moment, **Moz** *reaches into his pocket.*

Commentator He's reaching for a card. What colour will it be?

Moz *pulls out a set of keys.*

Moz Here y'are. Get yourself a set cut.

Billy A few weeks, lad! That's all!

Commentator It's yellow! He's a lucky lad!

Billy *takes the keys from* **Moz**, *then the* **Referee** *writes his name and number in his notebook.*

Fans (*sing*)
    Outside the Shankly Gates
    I heard a Kopite calling
    Shankly, they have taken you away
    But you left a great eleven
    Before you went to Heaven
    Now it's glory round the Fields of Anfield Road.

With play back under way, the **Everton Striker** *wins possession from the* **Liverpool Midfielder** *and switches it to* **Billy**. **Billy** *runs at the* **Liverpool Full Back**. *The* **Liverpool Full Back** *backs off and backs off, but tries desperately to keep his eye on the ball. As* **Billy** *shimmies one way, and then the other, he becomes:*

Nine EVERTON 1 − LIVERPOOL 1

Billy, *aged twenty-five, standing on the edge of the pitch at Anfield in the close season. He watches as* **Bill Sr** *takes handfuls of grass seed from his pockets and sprinkles them over the soil, while humming a tune.*

Billy Dad?

Bill Sr *is listening to a Walkman via some headphones and hasn't noticed* **Billy**'s *arrival. He carries on sprinkling the seeds until, eventually,* **Billy** *catches his eye:*

Bill Sr Billy! (*Beat.*) What are . . . are you here cos o' . . . ?

Billy I thought I'd just . . . y'know.

Bill Sr Aw, I'm made up you've, er . . . I really am. (*Beat.*) I've found a tape of her − that's what I was −

Billy A tape of me mum?

Bill Sr Yeah. At a gig. Singin'. How about that, eh?

Billy Where d'yer find it?

Bill Sr Well, I'd started to . . . I mean, there's tons o' stuff, ain't there? And I thought maybe it was about time I . . . but I got to this and that was that. Y'know, if you ever wanted to have a look through, then . . . well, it's −

Billy Nah.

Bill Sr Right. OK. Yeah.

Pause. **Billy** *looks out across the pitch.*

Billy Looks funny with no grass, doesn't it? Doesn't look right.

Bill Sr Look beautiful come August.

Billy S'pose so, yeah.

Bill Sr Doesn't seem like seventeen years, does it?

Billy Does to be honest, yeah.

Bill Sr I know, but not seventeen.

Billy   Seems like more.

Bill Sr   Time gets funny as yer get older, mate, you'll find that – I'm not bein' a wise old fart. Just does. Years last decades when you're a kid, don't they? But when you get to my age they take a month or two at most. Without a footie season I wouldn't know where I was, honest to God. Yer get bigger, yer get stronger, yer know more stuff, yer fall in love and it goes to shite, yer get a job, yer meet more people, yer fall in love again and it . . . goes alright. And then . . . one day yer realise that nothin'll ever happen to yer for the first time ever again. But yer hold on for those small victories. So small that other people could be in the same room when they happen . . . and not even notice.

Billy (*beat*)   Can I have a listen?

Bill Sr   Yeah?

Billy *nods.* **Bill Sr** *rewinds the tape, then places the left earphone in his right ear and the right earphone in* **Billy**'s *left ear. He presses play. There is a pause and a crackle, then:*

Queen Jean (*sings*)
  Does anybody know how long to World War Three?
  I wanna know, I've gotta book me holidee
  They want me in the army, but I just can't go
  I'm far too busy listenin' to the radio.

It is not the strong soaring voice of before. The accent is thicker and it's slightly out of key. **Billy** *and* **Bill Sr** *stand in silence as they listen, but* **Billy**'s *breath starts to quicken.*

Queen Jean (*sings*)
  The whole thing's daft, I don't know why
  Yer have to laugh, or else yer cry
  Yer have to live or else yer –

Billy *pulls the earphone from his ear, and* **Bill Sr**'s *comes with it too – the singing stopping abruptly.*

Bill Sr   What d'yer do that for?

Billy   That's not her!

Bill Sr   Course it is.

Billy   Doesn't sound anythin' like her! That's just some . . . club singer!

Bill Sr   What were you expectin'? She was hardly Maria Callas, mate . . .

Billy   Mam sounded great!

Bill Sr   To us. To us.

Billy   They called her Queen Jean!

Bill Sr   She could be a bit grand . . .

Billy   She was gonna be famous!

Bill Sr   Nah.

Billy   She was a star!

Bill Sr   You were a kid, Billy.

Billy   I remember!

Bill Sr   Oh eh, Billy lad . . .

There is a pause, then **Billy** *tries to sell the dummy, but the* **Liverpool Full Back** *reads it to perfection and slides him into touch.*

Commentator   Great tackle! The young lad isn't having any joy at the moment!

Everton Boss   Don't overplay it, Billy!

Summariser   There's some movement on the bench. Might be changes on the way here.

Commentator   They wouldn't sub the sub, would they?

Summariser   Well, he does look tired. Sensational in the first half, but not the same player since the equaliser.

Billy *glances at the bench anxiously, and becomes:*

Ten   EVERTON 1 – LIVERPOOL 1

Billy, *aged twenty-six, carrying his holdall and walking across the park towards a woman sitting on a bench. It is* **Claire**. *She is watching two young* **Boys** *training: running from different directions, and leaping to head an imaginary ball, before landing, running again, turning, and doing the same thing once more.*

Billy   Claire Gibson? Hiya!

Claire   Billy Walters? Alright?

Billy   Elaine said you'd moved back round here.

Claire   Elaine?

Billy   Your best mate Elaine!

Claire   What? Elaine Cullen? From school?

Billy   Yeah. She's still with our Maurice, y'know.

Claire   Right. Right. (*Beat.*) It's been I-don't-know-how-many-years, hasn't it?

Billy   Thirteen.

Claire   Has it?

Billy   Yeah.

Fan (*shouts*)   Get back! Come on! Get back!

Billy *looks at the two* **Boys** *running, jumping, running, turning, running, jumping, running, turning.*

Billy   Yeah. Kids, eh? I was just like that. Grew up playin' on this park. (*Beat.*) It's so nice to talk to ya. (*Beat.*) We should have a d-d-drink sometime.

Claire   Oh no, Billy, I –

Billy   For old times!

Claire *shakes her head firmly. There is another pause, then:*

Billy   Yeah. I've got a couple of things actually.

Claire   Yer wha'?

As **Billy** *rustles in his holdall, one of the* **Boys** *gets distracted and starts to look over.* **Billy** *pulls a helium balloon and a half-flattened bag of candyfloss out of the bag and holds them up, smiling.* **Claire** *stares at them.*

Claire   What are yer doin'?

Billy   We never got to go Pleasureland, did we? Well, I thought – why don't I get Pleasureland to come to us?

Claire   Billy, it's been *years*!

Billy   Yeah. Thirteen. I said.

Claire   It's a lifetime ago!

Billy   I shoulda skipped trainin'. Shoulda give the match a miss.

Claire   Billy!

Billy   We could start again.

Claire   I'm married!

Billy   What?

Boy   Mam? Mam? Are youse alright?

Claire   Yeah, love. Fine. Keep playin'.

Billy   He's yours?

Claire   They both are.

Billy   Right.

Claire   They've just started playin' for your dad . . .

Billy *nods. Pause.*

Billy   D'yer think they'd like some candyfloss?

Claire   No.

Billy   No. OK. Right. Right.

The **Everton Boss** *raises his arm.* **Billy** *holds his breath. The* **Everton Boss** *beckons the* **Everton Striker** *over.* **Billy** *breathes out, then hands the balloon and the candyfloss to the* **Everton Boss**.

Commentator   And Walters is staying on. He's still got a chance to influence this game, but he really needs to find something from somewhere . . .

The **Everton Striker** *and the* **Liverpool Midfielder** *are substituted, and the* **Liverpool Substitute** *and the* **Everton Substitute** *run onto the pitch. Play is resumed as the* **Liverpool Full Back** *kicks the ball high into the air.*

Everton Substitute   Heads up!

Billy   Mine!

Billy *follows the ball across the sky, then leaps to head it and becomes:*

Eleven   EVERTON I – LIVERPOOL I

Billy, *aged twenty-seven, looking up at the sky from the top of a tree in the park. He is clearly under the influence of alcohol.*

Billy   Yer gave a kid six grand a week! (*Beat.*) What did you expect?

There is a pause, then – despite his best efforts – **Billy** *starts to slide down the tree, before falling to the ground.*

Summariser   Beaten to the header easily.

Everton Boss   Get up, Billy! Get up!

As **Billy** *lies on the ground, the* **Referee** *and the* **Liverpool Substitute** *leap over him, and he becomes:*

Twelve   EVERTON I – LIVERPOOL I

Billy, *aged twenty-eight, lying on the living-room floor in* **Moz** *and* **Elaine's** *house. He sits up and holds his head for a second – then something catches his eye. It's his football. He crawls over to it, then picks it up carefully, and stands. He holds it out in front of him as if it's Yorick's skull, and stares at it with wonder.*

Billy   Billy Walters Walks on Water. Billy Walters Walks on Water. You can do it Billy. You can. One day you'll score the winner in the derby.

Around him, the **Everton Substitute** *tries to win possession back from the* **Liverpool Full Back** *and the* **Liverpool Substitute**. **Billy** *looks at them, then puts the football down delicately, and leaps back into the action. As he tears from player to player, he becomes:*

Thirteen   EVERTON I — LIVERPOOL I

Billy, *still aged twenty-eight, sprinting through the park. He slides into a tackle on the* **Liverpool Substitute**, *then starts to do sit-ups.*

Commentator   Walters is getting stuck in here. He's really putting himself about again.

Billy *leaps up, dives into a tackle on the* **Liverpool Full Back**, *then starts to do press-ups.*

Summariser   Looks like he's got second wind . . .

The ball runs loose to the **Everton Substitute**, *who back-heels it to* **Billy**. *The* **Liverpool Substitute** *starts to back away from him, the* **Referee** *in close attendance.*

Commentator   He's in a bit of space!

Summariser   The sub's backing off!

There is a pause, then **Billy** *take a cigarette pack from his pocket. He takes a cigarette from it and stares at it for a moment before lighting it.*

The **Liverpool Substitute** *and the* **Referee** *stay focused on the ball.*

Commentator   Well, would you look at that!

Summariser   There's no shortage of confidence with this kid!

Billy *takes a long drag from the cigarette, then stubs it out, and goes to continue his run. However, the* **Liverpool Substitute** *times his challenge to perfection. As* **Billy** *sprawls across the turf, he becomes:*

Fourteen   EVERTON 1 – LIVERPOOL 1

Billy, *aged twenty-nine, clutching his football and scribbling on a piece of paper in the living room of* **Moz** *and* **Elaine**'s *house.* **Moz** *and* **Elaine** *sit either side of him. There is clearly tension in the room.*

Elaine   Are yer goin' out tonight, Billy?

Billy   No way. I can't.

Elaine   I'll shout you a tenner.

Moz   Elaine . . .

Elaine   I will.

Billy   I'm writin' letters.

Moz   Who to, mate?

Billy   To clubs. I'm gonna start playin' again.

Elaine   Football?

Billy   What else?

Moz   Are yis serious?

Billy   Why not?

Fans (*sing*)
   Who ate all the pies
   The burger and the fries
   You fat bastard, you fat bastard
   Who ate all the pies?!

Moz   It's been a long time.

Billy   I've got a long time left.

Moz   What about your knee?

Billy   It'll be alright.

Moz   How many letters are you writin'?

Billy   Ninety-two.

Elaine   Is that our printer paper?

Billy   I'll get it yer back. And more. You wait.

Moz   All ninety-two clubs?

Billy   Yeah.

Moz   Everton?

Billy   Yeah.

Moz   Liverpool?

Billy   I know I could still cut it. And you could be my assistant. And agent. And everythin'. Be the greatest comeback since Ali!

Moz *and* **Elaine** *look at each other. There is a pause, then* **Moz** *looks at* **Billy** *again.*

Moz   You're handwritin' 'em?

Billy   Eh?

Moz   You're handwritin' the letters?

Billy   Yeah.

Elaine   Billy, they'll . . . they'll think it's like a kid or somethin'. You can't handwrite 'em, Billy.

Billy   It's not about how I write, it's about how I play.

Moz   Mate . . .

There is a pause as **Billy** *stops, reads back what he's written, then screws the letter up and starts on a fresh piece of paper, before thumping the turf.*

Billy   Foul, referee!

Referee   Got the ball!

Commentator   Wonderful challenge . . .

The **Liverpool Substitute** *draws the* **Everton Substitute***, then plays a ball wide for the* **Liverpool Full Back** *to chase, and hurtles down the middle for the return.* **Billy** *leaps up and tries to catch the* **Liverpool Full Back** . . .

Summariser   The sub's in miles of space in the middle! Walters needs to win this!

The **Liverpool Full Back** *slightly overruns the ball. As both he and* **Billy** *lunge in desperately in an attempt to win it,* **Billy** *becomes:*

Fifteen   EVERTON 1 − LIVERPOOL 1

Billy, *still aged twenty-nine, searching through the large box with 'Jean's stuff' written on it as* **Bill Sr** *enters.*

Bill Sr   Billy?

Billy   I've just come round to collect some stuff.

Bill Sr   Your mam's stuff?

Billy   Yer said I could? Don't yer remember?

Bill Sr   I said you could look through it.

Billy   I have done. I'm takin' this.

Bill Sr   Why didn't you come round when I was in?

Billy   I didn't know you were gonna be out.

Bill Sr   I coach Tuesdays and Thursday. You know that.

Billy   I'd forgotten.

Bill Sr   Every other single night I'm in. (*Beat.*) What yer gonna do with it?

Billy   There's no point it bein' in a cupboard, is there? Doin' not'in. Might be able to . . . get some decent cash for this. (*Beat.*) Eh? Why not? (*Beat.*) What? What? What's wrong with you? (*Beat.*) You said I could. You said. (*Beat.*) Why not, eh?

Fan (*shouts*)   What are yer doin', eh? What are yer doin'?

Bill Sr   What are you doin' with your life, Billy?

Billy   What are yer talkin' about?

Bill Sr   Come home, lad.

Billy   This isn't home.

Bill Sr   Come home and start again. You could go to college, you could –

Billy   Why would I start again?

Bill Sr   Mate, life after footie is hard. I know that as much as anyone.

Billy   But I'm not *after* footie. I'm *during* it. I'm trainin'. And Moz is puttin' a word in for me. He knows someone at Burscough. I mean, Bestie played for Dunstable, didn't he? Just need to get back on the pitch. Just need to show what I can do.

Bill Sr   Oh, Billy. *(Beat.)* I've been lucky to stay in the game.

Billy   Stay in the game? You're not in football – you're in gardenin'!

Bill Sr   I meant the coachin'.

Billy   Workin' with kids? That don't make you a coach – makes you a red coat!

Bill Sr *(beat)*   You should come down and coach with me. We've got three age bands now. You could. You could come down and learn from me.

Billy   Are you jokin'? What could I possibly learn from you?

Bill Sr   The basics.

Billy   Did you play in the derby, eh? Did yer?

Bill Sr   That was ten years ago!

Billy   But I'm comin' back, aren't I? That's what I said! And besides – I quit out o' choice. Did you?

Bill Sr   I quit cos of you!

Billy   Me?

Bill Sr   What choice did I have? I had to move back here! I couldn't even play away! Without you, I could've played on for years!

Billy   For what? Eh? Scrapin' around the lower leagues, a few games here, a few games there. Never in the same position. A clogger. A journeyman. D'you know what my mates used to say? D'you have any idea how humiliatin' it was for me?

Bill Sr   Well, is it anythin' like I feel now? Seein' you. Thievin' your mam's stuff!

Billy   Thievin'? I'm not thievin'!

Bill Sr   Was it anythin' like that?

Billy   You quit cos o' me? Well, sorry, my apologies. But if you blame me for murderin' your career, you're wrong – it wasn't a murder, it was a mercy killin'!

Bill Sr   Tell ya this, lad, if I'd've had your talent I'd've captained England!

Billy   Well, ya didn't! So if I wanna know about lawn-mowin', then I'll come to you!

Bill Sr   I know football!

Billy   What? Showin' eight-year-olds how to kick straight? For nothin'? Not a penny?

Bill Sr   You really don't know the first thing about it. Don't think you ever did.

Billy   Ha!

Bill Sr   The game you know and the game I know have nothin' in common.

Billy   The game changed!

Bill Sr   No! You did! It's not about Premier League. Or Champions League. Or Sky Sports. Or Transfer Windows. Or Signin'-on Fees. Or the Thirty-Ninth Game. Or Image Rights. Or WAGs. Or LTDs. Or Escape Clauses. Or Bosmans. Or Prozone. Or PLCs!

Billy   So tell me then! Go on! Tell me!

Pause.

Bill Sr   Toffs made the rules up, y'know. Was them what
stopped you bein' able to catch it. Or kick or shove each other.
They made the game a game of skill and they did it to teach
the workers a sportin' lesson. The toffs was the very first
dribblers. And they started the FA Cup just so's they could
show off their skills. And the toff who got the ball would run
with it and beat man after man till he either scored or was
tackled. And whoever tackled him'd do the same. (*Beat.*) Then
one particular year they played this team o' Lancastrians. A
team o' plumbers and weavers. A team who hardly had any
time to practise. A team who worked all day every day. And
the toffs couldn't wait! (*Beat.*) But somethin' happened. The
workers weren't well read. They hadn't heard of individualism.
No one had explained it to 'em. All they knew was solidarity.
So they passed the ball. Not one of 'em dribbled. They passed.
And moved. And passed. And moved. And passed! And moved!
And passed! And moved! And they won! They won the cup!
And I tell ya this, Billy. Forget what anyone else says, what
anybody claims, football was invented there and then. And if
there's one thing worth believin' in in this tight-arsed bastard
of a world, then it's that. It's that. (*Beat.*) Your problem was . . .
you never learnt to pass.

There is a pause, then **Billy** *and the* **Liverpool Full Back** *crash
into each other at full pelt and fall to the ground. Both roll round in agony,*
Billy *clutching his knee.*

Commentator   I think they're both hurt there!

Summariser   A reckless challenge! They've injured
themselves!

Commentator   Walters looks in a bad way!

Summariser   And the Liverpool player's through!

Billy   Kick it out! Stop play! Referee!

As the **Referee** *signals to play on,* **Billy** *becomes:*

Sixteen   EVERTON 1 — LIVERPOOL 1

Billy, *still aged twenty-nine, reading a copy of* Roy of the Rovers *in the spare room at* **Moz** *and* **Elaine**'s *house. He pulls the comic closer to him. There is a pause, then* **Hardman Johnny Dexter** *and* **Blackie Gray** *appear and move through the frames of the comic strip once more.*

Billy   Blackie! Hardman! (*Thinks.*) But where's . . . ?

As they move into the next frame, **Roy Race** *appears alongside them.*

Billy   Roy Race! (*Thinks.*) Hmm, I wonder if he still wants me to play for Melchester . . .

They move into the next frame.

Speak to me. Speak to me. Lads!

But **Roy Race**, **Hardman Johnny Dexter** *and* **Blackie Gray** *don't say a word. They move into the next frame.*

Billy   I can still play, y'know! I can . . .

Roy Race, **Blackie Gray** *and* **Hardman Johnny Dexter** *start to disappear.* **Billy** *turns over page after page – flicking frantically through the comic till he gets to the end, turns round and sees that they've gone. His head sinks, then he tries to get back to his feet. The* **Liverpool Full Back** *does likewise, while the* **Everton Substitute** *chases back, and the* **Liverpool Substitute** *looks up.*

Commentator   I think he's spotted the keeper off his line! He's not gonna have a go, is he?!

As the **Liverpool Substitute** *chips the ball towards the goal, all freeze, and* **Billy** *becomes:*

Seventeen   EVERTON 1 — LIVERPOOL 1

Billy, *aged thirty, entering the living room of* **Moz** *and* **Elaine**'s *house. On the floor are two plastic bags and a holdall. As* **Billy** *enters,* **Moz** *is putting his tool-belt on.*

Billy   Did you ask 'em, Moz? Did you ask for me?

Moz   Billy, look, we need to –

Billy   What are the bags for?

Fan (*shouts*)   Get him off, eh! Get him off the pitch!

Billy   Is that my stuff?

Moz   Bit awkward this, isn't it?

Billy   Are you kickin' me out?

Moz   No. No. As if.

Billy   Right.

Moz   It's just time you moved, innit?

Billy   Wha'?

Moz   I'm sorry.

Billy   Is it Elaine?

Moz   No.

Billy   It is. I know it is.

Moz   It isn't.

Billy   It is.

Moz   It's me! (*Beat.*) I'm turnin' into me dad, Billy. Me and Elaine, that's how it's goin'. And I couldn't do nothin' about it when I was a kid. I couldn't make 'em get on. I tried, and couldn't do a thing. But now I can. I wanna get things right. We both do. I want it to be possible to get things right.

Billy (*beat*)   You're sacked.

Moz   As what?

Billy   As me assistant.

Moz   Billy, I never was your assistant! I never was!

Billy   Then what were yer, eh? A kid who was forced to hang around with their cousin?

Moz No!

Billy You must think I'm stupid!

Moz That wasn't it!

Billy Then what?

Moz A friend!

Billy (*beat*) I let you live my life.

Moz Yeah. Well, I didn't like it. I prefer my own.

Billy *pulls* **Moz**'*s screwdriver from his tool-belt and waves it in his face.*

Billy What? This?

Moz Give it me back, Billy. I've got a job to do.

Billy Yer can forget Burscough, mate. I'll ask myself.

Moz Billy –

Billy And I won't be there for long.

Moz Billy, listen –

Billy Just the first step for me. First step on the road back!

Moz Billy, I asked! I asked!

Billy Well then. Well. You'll see. Just watch me go.

Moz It ain't gonna happen, Billy. You know it's not.

Billy What did they say?

Moz Just go, eh, mate.

Billy What did they say?!

Moz What d'yer think they said?!

Billy *points* **Moz**'*s screwdriver at him.* **Moz** *holds his hand out for it.*

Moz Look, just give us me screwie and be gone when I get back, eh?

Billy I haven't got anywhere else to go.

Moz *picks up* **Billy**'*s holdall and offers it to him.*

Moz   I've said I'm sorry.

Billy   Tell me what they said.

Moz   Billy . . .

Billy   Tell me!

Moz   They laughed, Billy! They laughed! They laughed cos your knee's gone. Cos your legs've gone. Cos your pace has gone. Cos you smoke. Cos you drink. Cos you're thirty years old. They laughed! They just laughed!

Billy *volleys one of the plastic bags and lashes out at the holdall with the screwdriver. There is a bursting sound.* **Moz** *drops the holdall.* **Billy** *stares at* **Moz** *with the screwdriver poised. There is the sound of hissing air.*

Moz   You've burst it.

Billy   What?

Puncture   Sssssssss . . .

Billy *listens to the sound for a moment.*

Billy   Oh, no . . .

Suddenly, **Billy** *drops to his knees, discards the screwdriver and unzips the holdall. He pulls out his football.*

Puncture (*louder*)   Sssssssss . . .

Billy   Oh, come on . . . eh . . . come on . . . come on . . .

He lifts the ball up and tries to blow air back into it with rapidly increasing desperation.

Please, just . . . eh . . . come on, just . . . eh . . .

Puncture (*louder*)   Sssssssss . . .

Moz   You can get footballs anywhere, Billy.

Billy   This was my . . . this was –

Moz   I was there, I . . . I read the card. All it said was –

Billy   It said –

Moz   'Happy Birthday, Billy. Dad.'

Commentator   It's there!

Summariser   What a finish!

As the **Crowd** *goes wild, the* **Liverpool Substitute** *drops to his knees and raises his arms. The* **Liverpool Full Back** *doesn't celebrate. He's still down, injured.* **Billy** *looks at the* **Referee** *and shakes his head slowly, but the* **Referee** *just points to the halfway line.* **Billy** *crumples over, the empty ball in his hands beneath him.*

Commentator   And what a turnaround we've seen here! It's now Everton, one – Liverpool, two!

The **Everton Boss** *turns and boots a water bottle, before sitting with his head in his hands.*

Summariser   And look at the Everton boss! He's distraught! The papers won't be kind to him tomorrow if it stays like this. He'll have to consider his position . . .

Commentator   Let's look at it again. Just watch the vision here . . .

Moz   They laughed, Billy! They laughed!

Commentator   And the chip . . .

Moz   'Happy Birthday, Billy. Dad.'

Commentator   Inch-perfect!

Billy *tries to get up, but his knee gives way. The* **Liverpool Full Back** *is struggling just the same. The* **Fourth Official** *holds up a board with a number 3 on it.*

Commentator   And the Fourth Official's indicating that there's only three more minutes to play. Is it too late for this Everton side now?

Summariser   There's two men down! I think Walters' knee's gone. Doesn't look good . . .

Commentator   Both teams have made all their substitutions!
Are they gonna have to see this game out with ten men?

Fans (*sing*)
  Go home
  You might as well go home
  You might as well go home!

As play gets under way again, and **Billy** *and the* **Liverpool Full
Back** *try to get back on their feet, everything starts to slow down, and
earlier moments appear around* **Billy**.

Bill Sr   I heard them chant your name. I heard it. I'm stood
there, no one around, and it hits me like a ball in the face.
What a game. What a game.

New Boss   Where will you be a few years down the line?

Agent   Who can you trust in this world, eh, Billy boy?

Bill Sr   Yer get bigger, yer get stronger, yer know more stuff,
yer fall in love and it goes to shite, yer get a job, yer meet more
people, yer fall in love again and it . . . goes alright. And then . . .

Moz   Here y'are, mate. Get yourself a set cut.

Bill Sr   Y'know, if you ever wanted to have a look through
then . . . well, it's –

Claire   A lifetime ago!

Elaine   Billy, they'll . . . they'll think it's like a kid or
somethin'. You can't handwrite 'em, Billy.

Bill Sr   And I tell ya this, Billy. Forget what anyone else says,
what anybody claims, football was invented there and then.

With a monumental effort, **Billy** *lets go of the deflated football and
finally stands up. He picks up his holdall and plastic bags and starts to
limp, painfully and heavily, across the pitch.*

Commentator   There's just seconds left, and this really has
been a typical derby match! Last-minute winners and –

Summariser   Small victories. So small that –

Commentator   Other people could be in the same room when they happen . . .

Commentator *and* **Summariser**   And not . . . even . . . notice.

Fans (*sing*)
Walk on through the wind
Walk on through the rain
Though your dreams be tossed and blown.

As the **Fans** *sing,* **Billy** *becomes:*

Eighteen   EVERTON I − LIVERPOOL 2

Billy, *still aged thirty, entering the living room of the Walters' flat.* **Bill Sr** *looks round and sees him. There is a pause, then:*

Bill Sr   Billy, what are yer . . . ?

Billy *drops his bags and gets the Subbuteo set from the corner of the room. He drops to his knees and starts to set up the goalposts, stands, floodlights and everything.*

Bill Sr   Billy?

Billy   I wanna do the derby. I wanna do that derby again . . .

Fans (*sing*)
Walk on, walk on
With hope in your heart
And you'll never walk alone.

Billy   Will yer give us an 'and settin' up?

Bill Sr *doesn't move, just watches − frozen to the spot.*

Billy   Have a game with me then. Please. Just have a game o' Subbuteo with me. Please.

Pause.

Bill Sr   Bagsies red . . .

Bill Sr *crouches down next to* **Billy** *and carefully they start to construct the match together. As they do, the* **Referee** *jumps onto his base, and the* **Subbuteo Referee** *puts the whistle to his lips.*

Commentator   Looks like the referee's about to blow! This could be it!

Fans (*sing*)
   You'll never walk alone . . .

The **Liverpool Substitute** *and the* **Everton Substitute** *leap back onto their bases too. And, as the* **Subbuteo Referee** *blows his whistle and the* **Crowd** *roars,* **Billy** *and* **Bill Sr** *look at each other.*

Bill Sr   Right?

Billy   Right!

The flick their **Subbuteo Footballers** . . .

Full-time.

Post-Match

Around the performance space, the post-match phone-in from a local radio station plays.

Outside the performance space, the **Street Evangelist** *continues to speak to members of the* **Crowd** *while pacing up and down the pavement with the banner proclaiming, 'Prepare To Meet Thy God'.*

Street Evangelist   Many are called, but few are chosen! Many are called, but few are chosen!